# The BEAUTIFUL NATURECRAFT BOOK

# The BEAUTIFUL NATURECRAFT BOOK

STERLING
PUBLISHING CO., INC.
NEW YORK

First published in the United States of America in 1979 by
Sterling Publishing Co., Inc., Two Park Avenue,
New York, N.Y. 10016
Published in Canada by Saunders of Toronto, Ltd.

This arrangement and adaptation
copyright ©1979 Search Press Limited, London

ISBN 0–8069–5388–8 Trade
     0–8069–5389–6 Library

Phototypeset in Great Britain by A. Brown & Sons, Hull,
and printed in Spain by Editorial Elexpuru Hnos,
Zamudio–Bilbao

## Acknowledgments

Some of the photographs and drawings in
Naturecraft were first published in the Leisure
Crafts series by Search Press, 2/10 Jerdan
Place, London, SW6 5PT.

The objects, drawings and texts are by the
following:
Caroline Agar
Diethold Buchheim
Lothar-Günther Buchheim
Richard Cory
Peter Dufour
Ruth Dürr
Doris Epple
Hans Fasold
Maxine Fitter
Richard Fox
Willi Harwerth
Doris Hazzard
Katinka Hendrichs
Ludwina Korselt
Jet Kuyvenhoven
Bunty Miller
Ruth Phelps
Polly Pinder
Käthe Schnierle
Arthur Schulz
John Smith
Margaret Smith
Paul Terry
Hans Thiel
John Turk
Shirley Turk
Michael Woods
Pamela Woods

The photographs are by the following:
Robert Harding
Hawkley Studios
Jan den Hengst
Jeet Jain
John Morfett
Toni Schneiders

# Introduction

If you have ever been for a walk in the countryside in sun, wind or rain you can't have failed to notice all that happens season by season to flowers, plants, trees, stones or earth, by seashore or river bank or field. You might suddenly notice how pebbles that are usually dull and ugly, gleam and shine when they are wet with rain or sea water. If you look at them closely you will see that they are full of the most marvelous colors that you have failed to notice before. But it's not just the colors that make natural objects so attractive, it's textures of surfaces, shapes, patterns, size whether large or tiny, and the harmony with which all these things go together.

When you start collecting stones, shells, feathers, dried flowers, leaves, driftwood or seed heads and bring them all home, you will very soon have the best part of a natural haystack in the back room! In order to bring out the best qualities from all of these natural objects, you need to instill your own creative designs into them. Make a start by trying a few stone figures: never mind painting them to begin with. Or design some simple leaf animals or seed pictures, or simply look more closely at that piece of driftwood and try to imagine what sculptural possibilities it has, and how it will look when cleaned and polished.

This book shows you how to make a whole range of different crafts with natural objects. Once you have made a start with some of the very effective and yet simple-to-do crafts, this book will help you work through to more complicated projects such as making corn dollies or mounting polished pebbles.

The color photographs show finished designs and creations that can be made up with help from directions in the text and captions. You can vary all these projects, of course, making them to your own design and color preferences and using materials that are readily available to you. At the beginning of each section there is a list of tools and materials you will need before you can begin work. Very few of these tools or materials are expensive, hard to find or difficult to use. In a short time you will find you have collected a basic tool kit and enough materials to manage most of these natural crafts. When using special glues or paints, always follow the manufacturer's instructions very carefully: all glues are for sticking, but each one has a different method of use. A glue used wrongly could cause a piece of craftwork to fall apart after a while.

Natural crafts vary in their uses. Some, such as feather flowers, are purely for decoration, while others, such as simple prints, can be used to enhance practical objects or to make greetings cards that can be sent to friends. But best of all, natural craftwork can make excellent gifts. For example, a bracelet of polished pebbles or a shell picture would make a very unusual and striking gift for Christmas or a birthday.

The whole natural world is full of objects just waiting to be seen, collected and used in your own craft designs. So why not start creating works of art yourself, right now!

# Contents

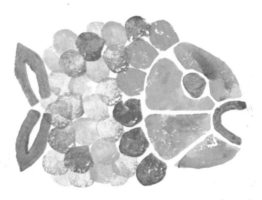

**Flower Arrangements**      **Page 58**

There is nothing difficult about arranging flowers. All you need is patience, care and imagination.

**Stone on Stone**      **Page 76**

Delightful little stone figures and animals are easy for you to make from beach pebbles or garden stones.

**Corn Dollies**      **Page 90**

You can make beautiful designs in straw and ribbon, by practicing this old, traditional, country craft.

**Weathered Wood Sculpture Page 100**

Old wood, from the land or seashore, can be turned into beautiful, unusual and artistic sculptures and decorations.

**Pressed Flowers**      **Page 66**

Collect, press and preserve spring and summer leaves and flowers. Use them on mats or cards and to make pictures.

**Dried Flowers and Seeds**      **Page 82**

Collect and dry summer flowers and seeds, and you can spend winter making lively and attractive decorations.

7

# Shellcraft

At one time or another, nearly everyone will have come home from a sea-side holiday with pockets bulging with beautiful shells collected from the beaches. So often, once at home the shells are put away and forgotten, yet with a little time, patience and imagination, sea shells can be made into attractive and unusual items to decorate the house. This is a fascinating hobby which will give hours of enjoyment through the dark winter evenings.

If you have access to a shell shop you will find that shells from all over the world are available, but if not, you can look forward to collecting

*Shells from all over the world.*

*The shell flower below is made from mussels, with a center made from a winkle shell. When making a flower as thick as this, mark the outline of the flower on the background by laying out the bottom circle of shells first.*

*This scorpion needs 23 tower or screw shells of different lengths for legs. It has a clam shell for the body and a small scallop shell for the head. The eyes are two small sea snail shells. It is glued with a two-part epoxy resin adhesive. When making up the legs, support them with non-hardening modeling clay, until the glue is dry. After assembly, give the sting and the pincers a second gluing for extra strength.*

some from the beaches on your next holiday and have the pleasure of working with the free raw material nature has provided.

Most shellcraft can be achieved by gluing. It is only in advanced work that shells need to be drilled or cut, so there is no complex or expensive equipment for the beginner to buy.

It is useful to know a little about the shells you collect, even though you are to use them purely for decoration. Borrow or buy a book and find out about them. Bivalves, such as mussels, are plentiful, and they are useful as fillers. Other bivalves are cockles, which vary in color from white to deep yellow, and tellins, which are wonderful for making flowers and butterflies. Clams are rather similar to tellins, and are splendid for petals. Univalves, such as periwinkles, are found in rock pools, as are shiny cowries, long, pointed turritellas and spiraled whelks. Different names are often used for the same shell, so try to find out what your supplier calls each one. For instance angels' wings are piddocks, babies' fingernails are tiny pink tellins and tower shells are turritellas.

As a useful reference make a sampler of shells, mounting a specimen of each shell on

*The fish on the left has been made in a frame backed with a board. The front is then filled with white cellulose plaster about 5mm ($\frac{1}{4}$ in.) thick, into which the shells are pressed, one by one.*

cardboard, with its name and habitat printed underneath.

*Collecting live shells*

When you are collecting shells, take plastic bags, tissues and plastic boxes with you in which to put your more delicate finds, as they break very easily.

Some shells can be cut in half to show their attractive inner shapes, but you may find some damaged or water-worn shells which are just as interesting. If you do, gather these with the whole shells. This will both save time in cutting and add variety to your work.

Try not to take home a shell complete with its inhabitant, as this will make the whole collection smell. If you do so by chance, either throw out the shell or boil it in a pan full of water to kill the mollusk, and then clean it with lukewarm, soapy water. Store clean, dry shells in plastic bags, boxes or discarded household containers.

When starting to work, give yourself plenty of room, with space to lay out the shells as well as an area in which you can leave things undisturbed overnight until the glue sets.

*Materials*

Most things needed are available from local

*The white flower above is made from sawtooth shells, with a winkle in the center.*

craft shops or florists' shops. Basic requirements are:

*Adhesive*. A clear, fast-drying glue. (Apply with a matchstick on small areas).

*Filler*. There are many all-purpose cement-type fillers on the market, useful for embedding shells on surfaces and for joining shells. They can be tinted with water paints.

*Jewelry findings*. Attachments, such as brooch backs and link rings, from craft shops.

*Varnish*. A little clear varnish will bring out the colors in shells, but never use too much as this might give the shells a yellow tinge, which is very unattractive.

*Paints*. The lovely natural colors of shells rarely need painting, but you may need to match one shell with another, in which case use water-color paints applied with a small brush.

*Additional materials for flowers*
*Green plastic-coated wire*. For stems.
*Silver-colored reel wire, or fishing line*. For delicate stems.
*Florist's tape*. To cover wires.
*Buttons*. For mounting shell petals.
*Tweezers*. For picking up tiny shells.

*These two fishermen are quite easy to make. They are sitting on oyster shells and each has a flat shell for a cap. Patience and care will be needed when arranging the arms and fishing rods to make sure the balance is correct. The rods are made from straw with a thread or wire glued inside the top.*

*Decorated boxes like this are the most popular of all shell work.*

*Jam jars.* To support buttons in flower making.
*Tissues.* To support buttons.
*Scissors and wire cutters.*

### Making shell designs
*Shell boxes*
Wooden boxes are best for decorating (see above). Do a practice design on a board first, to make sure you have sufficient shells to cover the whole box. Sandpaper the box until you have a smooth surface, then, working on one side of the box at a time, cover it with glue or a layer of filler and, starting from the center, work your design. A light coat of varnish when the box is finished will bring out the colors.

Leave a space along the hinged edge or the shells will shatter when the box is opened.

*Shell figures*
These are pretty combinations of all kinds of shells. Use the pictures on pages 13 and 14 to give you inspiration for your own figures. On the whole, shell figures look better without painted faces, though you can add a few features in watercolor paints if you feel it necessary. You can also make a discreet

12

*A dancer and a piper: carefully designed and skillfully glued, leaving almost no traces of adhesive at all.*

addition of a piece of wool or string here and there to represent hair. Some people prefer simply to glue the shells to each other, but if you want to strengthen the joints, you can join shells with a small pad of filler, then go over the whole joint with a clear glue when it has set hard.

### Shell animals

All sorts of strange animals can be made easily from shells, using glue, filler and paste.

Lay out the shells and see what sort of animals they suggest, then stick them together in these shapes. Look at the pictures here and use your own shells to make something similar.

### Shell jewelry

You can buy jewelry findings such as brooch backs and earring bases from most craft shops, and arrangements of small shells (like those on page 15) can be glued on these bases.

Choose your shells carefully, making sure to match them to produce pleasing, symmetrical patterns. After gluing, varnish each shell lightly to bring out its natural colors.

*Shell flowers*

These are perhaps the most beautiful of all designs you can make with shells, and from this very simple basic method you can go on to make many other, much more complex, stemmed flowers later.

1. Cut one length of green plastic-coated wire for each flower. Allow about 300 mm (12 in.) per stem, as it is easier to cut a wire short when arranging than it is to add a piece.

2. Attach the wire to a button by threading it through the holes and twisting the short end tightly round the longer end just below the button (see fig 1).

3. Place the button on a tissue held taut over a jam jar with an elastic band and insert the stem through the tissue, bending up the wire if necessary (see fig 2).

4. Glue the button and arrange four to six matching shells round it so that the shells just touch and make a petal formation. Stick a small top shell to the center of the flower.

Make sure that the shells you use are all the same size and note the direction in which they face: they should all be facing the same way. As most shells have more color and pattern on one

*A simple and enchanting Japanese shell lady.*

*A bullfight! The bull's head and body are made from a small and a large mussel shell, and the tail is teased-out coarse string. Legs and arms are screw shells.*

*The matador's feet need to be glued firmly to the shell base first. Make the figure up in stages, using non-hardening modeling clay for support wherever necessary.*

*Small arrangements of shells made up for use as pendants or brooches.*

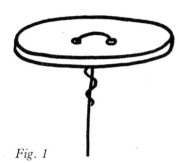

Fig. 1

Fig. 2

Fig. 3

Fig. 4

side than the other, choose the best colored shells for your work.

To cup petals, hollow the tissue and rest the button at the bottom of this, so that the sides of the tissue support the shells while the flower dries. The size and depth of the hollow will dictate the tightness of the cup. (See fig 3).

If multiple layers of shells are to be used, or if the button itself is pretty enough to be used as the center, an ideal way to begin is to place the button face down on the table with its stem supported in a jar of sand (see fig. 4) and glue the shells round this. Another way of making shell flowers is to place a small blob of filler or thick adhesive on a sheet of tissue paper, set the shells in it to form a flower, and, when dry, peel off the paper.

## Varying your flowers

For a pink rose, use graded tellins or white and pink cockles, starting with bigger shells at the base of the button and building up gradually to the center with smaller ones. Support the inner shells with little rolls of tissue paper while the glue sets.

A fine daisy can be made from long white piddocks (angels' wings) with a yellow periwinkle as a center.

Large wedge shells or purple butterfly clams make very realistic pansies or violas. Only three are needed to make a flower, so choose two matching shells which face in opposite directions (they may be two halves of the same shell) and another shell of the same size. Glue them to the button with the pair at the top and the other shell below. Add a small shell to make the center. For different flower centers, mass many little tellins or yellow periwinkles in the middle of larger, contrasting shells.

*A colorful arrangement of shell flowers in a basket.*

16

*A full scale shell flower arrangement using dried leaves to complete the array.*

Other types of flowers can be made with damaged shells. Do this by threading thin reel wire (fishing line) through the holes, then binding the shells together in spray formations, and then on thicker stem wire.

Black periwinkles make good sprays of blackberries. Secure a cotton wool (absorbent cotton) bud to a loop of reel wire (fishing line), coat it with glue, and push it deep into the shell. Each blackberry must be bound to a stronger wire with the smallest at the tip and the largest at the bottom. Cover all the wires with florist's tape.

Many flowers can be made more realistic by adding small extra touches. For instance, when wiring buttons, thread some stamens (obtainable from crafts shops) through them. A few dried leaves add greatly to the charm of any shell flower arrangement.

To make artificial leaves, cut strips of green crêpe paper into five points, place them close under the button of the finished flower, and bind them in place with florist's tape or narrow strips of paper. A touch of glue will keep the leaves in place.

# Pebbles to Pearls

Few of us can resist picking up and turning over the lovely, smooth, sea-washed pebbles found on the beaches. Their shiny wetness and glowing colors are very attractive, and an excellent way of preserving these colors and tones is to polish them. They can then be used to create jewelry and ornaments for the home.

Pebble polishing is a very simple and rewarding craft in which the whole family can participate – children are keen pebble collectors – and because the raw materials are free for the finding, it is an inexpensive pastime too. If you do not have a good natural source of

*A pestle, with a mortar filled with stones, is a marvelous way of displaying a mass of highly polished pebbles. Most of these are from the carnelian or agate group.*

*One beautifully polished carnelian stone set into the clasp of an old brooch.*

*A large polished pebble has been cut in half and glued to the center of this Maltese cross.*

pebbles near you, or you dont want to buy a tumble-polisher, you can buy stones cheaply, both polished and unpolished, from gem shops. When you first start this hobby, nearly all pebbles and stones will interest you, but with experience you will become more discerning in your choice, and pick up only those which you know will polish well.

### Hunting grounds

Almost all beaches are ideal hunting grounds, for the pebbles there are tumble-polished by nature and when wet, give a good idea of how they will look after polishing. Tidal shores provide a rich array of stones at low water, and rivers, mountain streams and even your own back garden are also good sources of material. Observe the basic safety rules when hunting for rocks and stones on beaches, taking care not to let the tide cut you off, and ask permission before venturing on private property. An excellent way of finding good collecting places is to join a local lapidary club and go on field trips with them.

### Tips on collecting

Hard stones usually polish up best of all. Because of their hardness, the many varieties of quartz pebbles and stones are most suitable for polishing. Flawless crystals of quartz, which occur in a wide variety of colors, are cut and polished and sold as gemstones.

Nothing is more depressing than collecting a heavy load of stones and finding that only a few are suitable for polishing. As a simple on-the-spot test to check for polishing potential, try scratching a pebble, first with a fingernail, then with a penknife, and then with a steel file. Harder minerals such as quartz will not mark, and, generally speaking, the weaker the mark made, the harder the stone is.

Pebbles found on beaches vary greatly in suitability for tumble-polishing.

Sandstone crumbles easily and is extremely porous, so it is not to be recommended at all. Sandstone-lined stones in the quartz-veined category look attractive with their striped effect, but on closer examination, you will see that the softer sandstone is fractionally con-

*An ugly looking geode, when cut in half reveals a wonderful center of sparkling macro crystals.*

cave, leaving the harder quartz vein raised.

Chalk is very soft, textured with millstone deposits, and usually contains fragments of marine life. Shale is composed of clay rocks and sometimes has close-bedded planes in parallel layers, so it does not polish well.

Geodes are unsuitable for polishing too. These almond-shaped rocks are found in volcanic regions. Hard and dull in appearance, they are often roughly textured. Small eruptions of quartz crystals on the surface indicate the possibility of a cavity in the center, and it is here that the spectacular looking crystals are massed. If you do find a geode, don't discard it. Ask a lapidary supplier to cut it in half so that its glistening crystal interior is exposed, and it

19

will make a beautiful and unusual ornament.

*What you need for polishing pebbles*
Electrically operated tumble-polisher
Three grades of grinding and polishing powder
Large sieve or colander
Basin or bucket
Small quantity of detergent powder
Plastic bags for sludge disposal
Pebbles and stones
Water

*What you need for making jewelry and ornaments*
Polished stones
Jewelry findings (i.e. attachments, from crafts suppliers or gem shops)
Small baking tray or tin lid
Sand or kitchen salt
Quick-setting epoxy resin
Tweezers
White spirit (alcohol) for cleaning surfaces
Tissue or rags
Small lid or foil container for mixing glue
Matchsticks for applying glue

A tumble-polisher is a revolving drum or barrel filled with grit which produces an abrasive action similar to that of sand and sea on pebbles. To get the best results from polishing, first you need attractively shaped and colored pebbles and secondly you need to pay careful attention during the various stages in the tumbling process.

Electrically operated tumble-polishers are obtainable from many crafts and gem shops in sizes that vary from 680g (1½ lb.) upwards. As they use very little power, they are not expensive to run. Silicone carbide is the

Below left: *The correct tumbling action should look like this. There should be a steady rumbling sound: if the sound is irregular, then add a few more stones.*

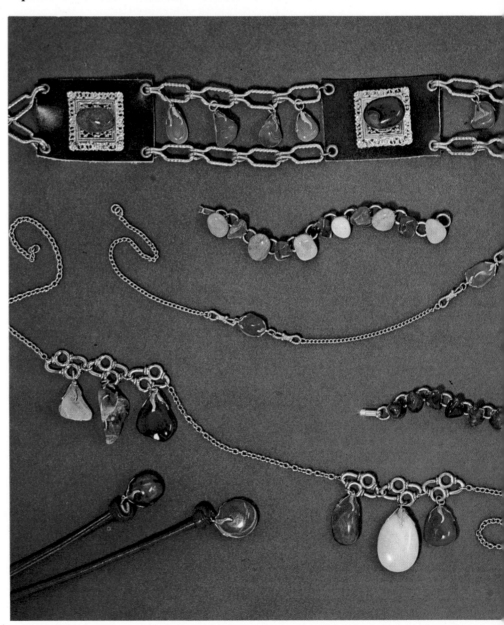

abrasive which smoothes the stones, and the addition of a polishing agent in the final stage ensures glossy pebbles. Ideally, all stones being polished together should be of the same hardness, because if you mix hard and soft, the softer ones may be completely ground away. Do mix pebble sizes though: small pebbles help in the tumbling as they grind into the hollows of the larger ones. However, no stone should be so large that it nearly fills the barrel. If you have a garage or a shed, put your tumble-polisher in there, away from the house, as the rumbling can be tiresome and the motor must be allowed to run day and night throughout the whole process. Should it remain stopped for any length of time, the grit and pebbles will settle and solidify and the stones will need to be freed from this cement-like mixture. Always stand a loaded barrel on its end when not in motion on the tumble-polisher.

Minor gases may be generated during tumbling, and if the barrel is not inspected daily pressure can build up, so that the cap is forced off. This is not dangerous, but it can be messy. So each day, check carefully, remove the cap, clean the thread well, and screw the cap back on tightly.

*Polishing pebbles – stage 1*
Wash the pebbles and place them in the barrel until it is about two thirds full. Then cover the stones with water. Add one part by weight of coarse no. 80 – 120 grit to eight parts by weight of stones. Close the lid firmly, place the barrel on the rollers, and switch on the power.

There should be a steady rumbling sound, which indicates that the stones are tumbling evenly. If the sound is irregular, the load is slightly light in stones, and a few more need to be added.

Smooth pebbles take up to a week of tumbling at this first stage, while very rough stones can take two to three weeks of continuous grinding. In this case there will be a gradual softening of the texture of the grit,

*Below right: Small pebbles help in the grinding as they get into the hollows between larger stones.*

*Below: Some excellent examples of the use of polished stones with existing metal jewelry.*

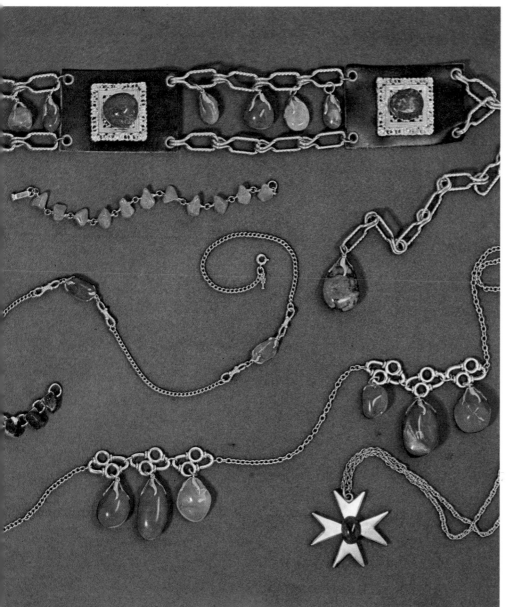

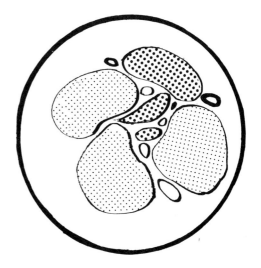

*This small ring has a carnelian set into the clasp.*

causing a thickening of the water and a less abrasive action, so the grit will need replenishing. Inspect the stones regularly, and when most of the rough edges have disappeared, pour the entire contents of the barrel into a colander or coarse sieve held over a large basin. Rinse the stones thoroughly into the basin. The sediment must *not* be poured into the household drains, as it will set like concrete and block them! If disposal is awkward, let the sludge settle in the basin overnight, drain off the liquid leaving the sediment on the bottom, place this in a plastic bag and throw it away.

*Stage 2*
Wash all stones very carefully and discard the chipped and pitted ones. They will not be wasted as they can be tumbled again from the start with rough stones. Make up the load to its original weight by adding some smooth, water-worn quartz pebbles. It is important that the added stones are of similar quality and texture to the others, so that polishing will be more or less uniform. Cover with water and add one part by weight of no. 220 – 320 grit to ten parts by weight of stones. Seal the barrel and tumble as before, inspecting at regular intervals.

(*Note.* This grind is optional and can be omitted if stage 1 has produced smooth pebbles.)

*Stage 3*

Drain as before, rinse and clean the barrel and stones. Cover with water and add one part by weight of no. 400 – 500 grit to ten parts by weight of stones. Tumble for another four to seven days, inspecting regularly.

The timing of this stage is determined by the finish on the surface of the stones after the four day period. After these three different grind-

ings, you should have a barrel full of smooth, refined stones.

*Stage 4*

Drain, rinse and clean the barrel and stones, and make sure the lid and sealing grooves are free from grit. It is very important at this stage to ensure that all traces of abrasive grit have gone. Reload the barrel and add two tablespoons of detergent powder. Cover with water and re-seal. Tumble for at least four hours. This cleans the pebbles beautifully, and saves you the task of washing each pebble separately.

*The wood-based necklace was made by first drilling small holes in the top of cross-section juniper disks. Connecting pieces of chain were glued into these holes and a fastener attached to either end. Light depressions were gouged out in each disk and a selection of chippings of polished stones glued on. The multicolored necklace was made from stones collected from all over the world, with findings glued to each end. The connecting rings were opened and closed with a pair of jewelry pliers. The fine gold strand necklace had one large carnelian added to it to make a pleasing piece of jewelry. The pair of earrings was made from equal size agates, each glued to a finding and bunched on a bar for pierced ears.*

23

Rinse thoroughly. Ideally, a separate barrel should be kept for this fine polishing stage.

Carefully replace the washed stones in the barrel and cover with water. Add about 225 g ($\frac{1}{2}$ lb.) of polishing agent such as tin oxide, cerium oxide, putty powder or levigated alumina. Seal the barrel and tumble.

If there is a loud swishing noise, you can add some small bits of material such as scraps of felt or leather, or even two teaspoons of wallpaper paste, to act as softeners. Run the tumbler for two to four days until you have really good shiny pebbles.

If there isn't a highly satisfactory shine at the end of this, repeat stage 3 and then repolish.

*Stage 5*
Drain the load and dispose of the sludge. Cover the stones with water and add two tablespoons of detergent. Tumble for eight to ten hours and rinse well.

*Quartzes suitable for tumbling*
Gemstone suppliers sell quartzes and minerals from all over the world.
Here is a list of quartzes suitable for tumbling.

*The pear tree was made from a branch off a pear tree, sprayed gold. The base was a thick mixture of plaster of paris sprayed gold when dry. A remnant of felt or velvet was stuck to the base to prevent scratching and slipping. Modeling clay was used for the partridge and this too was sprayed gold. Red beads were added for its eyes. Brass foil was used for the leaves, and veins were marked on each one. All the pears are polished carnelians attached with glue to findings. Fine fuse wire was used to attach these to the pear tree.*

*Carnelian*. Waxy appearance. Pale to deep red, smoky to pale yellow. Shows up well in sunlight. Translucent.

*Chalcedony*. Milky white to pale blue. Waxy in appearance. Transparent and sometimes opalescent.

*Moss agate*. Contains moss and fern-like deposits. Transparent to semi-transparent.

*Milky quartz*. Common as a beach pebble. White to creamy yellow. Opaque to translucent. Polishes well but must not be overheated.

*Banded quartz*. White through yellow to brown. The bands of crystalline are evident when cut and polished. Opaque to translucent.

*Conglomerates*. Round pebbles in a variety of color combinations. Opaque.

*Granite*. Common pebbles, in red and gray. Opaque.

*Marble*. Not advisable to polish this with other stones, but it is attractive set in jewelry. Opaque.

*Amber and jet*. Semi-precious materials of organic origin which polish well.

*Jet*. Found as water-worn pebbles and in seams on some coasts. Intense black. Opaque. Tough, but soft enough to carve.

*Amber*. Lightweight, and warm to the touch. Varies from pale yellow to dark red and sometimes contains fossilized insects and plants. Transparent to opaque. Too soft for the machine, polish by hand.

*Clear quartz* (rock crystal). Glassy, colorless.

*Citrine*. Amber to pale yellow. Could be mistaken for topaz. Transparent.

*Smoky quartz*. Varies from smoky yellow through brown to black. Often called cairngorm. Semi-transparent.

*Amethyst*. Varies from purple to pink, and sometimes has bandings of white and purple. Transparent to semi-transparent.

*Jasper*. Varies from red through brown-green to yellow. Can contain clear stripes and suspended particles. Polishes well.

*Agate*. Easily recognizable by banding and wide color range: brown, red, blue, yellow, pink and white. Carnelian and jasper agates occur too. Shows up well in sunlight. Semi-transparent or opaque.

*Flint*. Gray brown to black. Opaque.

### Tips on gluing

Most pebbles and stones are difficult to deal with, but a small baking tray and some sand or kitchen salt will make the task of setting them easier. Fill the tray with sand or salt and press down firmly. Press the pebbles into this and they will then be held fast while you attach the finding. With care, no grains will come into contact with the glue.

Don't leave the tray with gluing articles on it on the same bench as the tumbling machine; the vibrations could cause slipping.

Clean the pebbles with white spirit (alcohol) to make a better bond, before gluing. Fast-setting epoxy resins are best for gluing.

*A butterfly printed with card (pasteboard) and cardboard. Print the body and abdomen first, then add the basic wing shapes. The yellow on the wings is immensely effective: the butterfly would look much less attractive if it were just red and brown. Add the antennae and wing details last of all.*

*These faces, fish and flowers, and the train on the next page, were practice prints. They were printed with all the discarded pieces cut out from designs on larger potatoes. Each picture is made up from many small printings; this gives each one great detail and character. You can do really fine work more easily in this way, but you cannot make an identical shape a second time.*

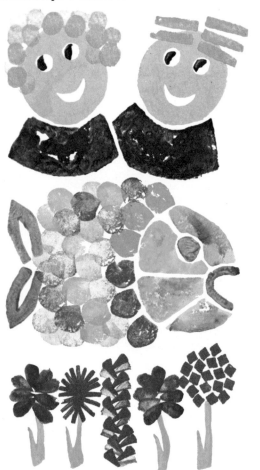

# Simple Printmaking

Printmaking with simple objects, without using expensive machinery or equipment, is both creative and fun to do. Prints can be made from almost any relief surface, such as fruit, vegetables, bobbins, string, leaves and combs. Prints can be made on a variety of papers and fabrics to create a whole range of attractive designs for use throughout the home.

## Making prints – color

The three primary or main colors are red, blue and yellow, and all other colors are made up from different mixes of these three primaries, from the most subtle or brilliant shades of green you see in the countryside to the swirling grays and blues of skies in the damp and misty months. From the three primary colors come the secondaries, purple (a mixture of red and blue), green (a mixture of yellow and blue), and orange (a mixture of red and yellow).

There are other colors which graduate between the primaries and the secondaries. If you add black to a color you get a tone; if you add white, a tint. The colors directly opposite each other on the color wheel are known as complementary colors, so that red is the complementary of green, yellow the complementary of purple, and blue the complementary of orange.

On the right is a basic color wheel (made with potato prints). The middle band of the wheel

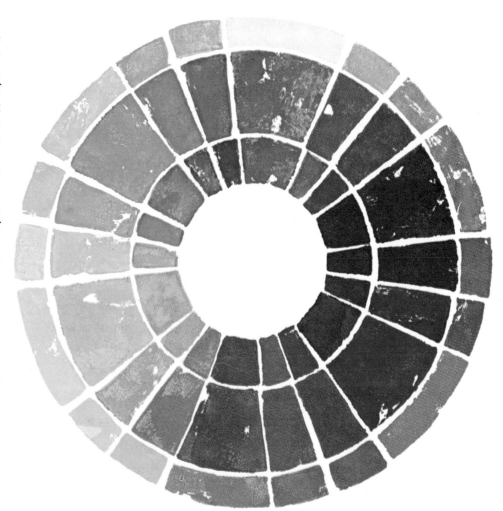

contains the three primary colors, the three secondary colors, and twelve graduated shades. By adding white to these colors you get the outer wheel of tints and by adding black you get the inner wheel of tones.

Experiment imaginatively with paints and/or inks until you find the colors and combinations of colors which you like, and with which you can make attractive designs.

### Making prints with potatoes

This is a very simple technique and an easy one to start with. You can use swedes (rutabagas) or turnips, as well as potatoes.

### Materials

You will need:

*Newspaper.* To cover the table top.

*Potatoes.* About four, scrubbed under a running tap to remove soil. The shapes don't

PAINT TOO THICK

PAINT TOO WATERY

UNEVEN SURFACE

*These potato prints can be used as guides to paint consistency and printing-surface quality.*

matter so long as they are easy to hold. Very old potatoes are not firm enough and tend to make prints with wavy edges, while very new potatoes retain moisture and make prints with watery looking colors.

*Cutting tools.* Use a sharp-pointed kitchen knife to cut images in the potatoes. A surgical or craft knife is useful for fine and detailed cutting. Crinkle-potato cutters will give potato halves an interesting surface, as will a grapefruit knife when scraped along the surface. Tiny cocktail or pastry cutters will produce more variations.

*Paint.* Any water-based paint, such as powder or block colors, poster paints or gouache.

*Brushes.* Two flat watercolor brushes, about 10 mm ($\frac{3}{8}$in.) wide, or a piece of sponge which can be held by a spring-type clothes peg (clothes pin). A fine brush (no. 4) is useful for detailed images.

*Palette.* A sheet of glass, laminated plastic or perspex about 230 × 180 mm (9 × 7 in.).

*Palette knife.* Buy this at an art shop.

*Water.* For cleaning brushes. Jam jars make good water pots, and you will need at least two.

*Paper.* Start with newsprint, cartridge paper (drawing paper), typing paper or colored sugar paper (construction paper).

*Apron.* To protect you from splashes.

*Rags.* An old sheet torn into squares makes good rags. Pin a rag to the table at your side so that you can wipe away any spilt paint instantly.

*How to work*

Cut the potato in half and wipe away any excess moisture with a clean rag. Don't cut an image into it just yet, but choose a color and paint it evenly across the potato surface using a brush or a piece of sponge. Now try printing.

The print may show that the paint on the potato was too thick or too watery or perhaps it may look blotchy, with areas on which there is no paint at all, which means the potato has an uneven surface. Try cutting another one in half, using an even sawing motion. Practice cutting and printing until you are satisfied with your prints, then start thinking about cutting an image.

*Coarse, colored potato prints drawn over to make animals.*

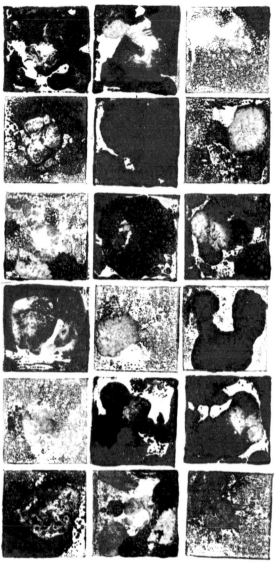

These few color patches printed with card (pasteboard) and oil- and water-based inks offer a wide range of shapes, tones, colors and patterns.

utility knife for detailed cutting. Try cutting a potato in half with a crinkle-potato cutter, and overprinting or twisting the image round slightly with each print. A grapefruit knife gives interesting textures: cut a potato in half, then run the grapefruit knife over the surface, digging in the serrated edge. This will give a print with fine lines. If the knife is scraped horizontally and vertically, the print will be made up of fine dots. (Some of the area may fill in with paint when you do this, but this will not necessarily spoil the finished printing effect.) Another tool for cutting an image is a small pastry cutter. Press the cutter as far into the potato as it will go, then pull it out and cut away the unwanted pieces of potato.

When experimenting with numbers and letters, remember you will need to cut some of

You can use a floral design like the one below on a greetings card, a table mat, as a print for a curtain (drape), or just as a picture in its own right. It has a wide range of colors and is made from a number of printings with small pieces of potato and cardboard.

Always leave enough potato to use as a handle. Never cut a very small image on a large piece of potato, as this will create problems when you want your prints to lie side by side.

Start with a simple image, like a U-shape. See how many different patterns you can make with it. If you print several times without renewing the paint on the potato, you will get paler tints and slightly different textures.

Now try cutting several different images, and also making prints with the pieces of potato cut out from your images. Remember that cut potato will not stay firm for very long, so you may have to cut the image again on another potato.

Experiment with using a surgical, craft or

the images the wrong way round. A will remain the same, for example, but B has to be reversed. Draw the letters lightly on the surface of the potato with a fiber-tip pen, and remove the ink gently with a damp cloth after the image has been cut.

*Paints, inks, papers and fabrics*
Many different paints and inks are suitable for printing. Water-based and oil-based printing inks are specially made for the purpose. The water-based ink is slightly better for detailed work than ordinary paints, and the oil-based ink gives even more detail for objects such as leaves and feathers. Use turpentine or the appropriate medium for cleaning off oil-based ink. Acrylic paint is good for fine work too, but it dries very quickly and is hard to remove from brushes if they are not washed immediately. Striking effects can be achieved with water- and oil-based inks by printing with different flat surfaces, including plastic or metal. The butterfly at the beginning of the chapter and the abstract on the previous page were printed with card (pasteboard) and cardboard.

Different types of paper give interesting textures – newspaper, embossed wallpaper, tissue, greaseproof paper, brown wrapping paper, all react differently to the same print. Even nappy (diaper) liners, with their delicate semi-transparent finish, make excellent wall-hangings!

Fabric printing is fun, and just as easy as printing on paper. You can brighten up T-shirts and dresses, or print on a full length of material and then make up original garments.

*A good example of a beautiful print made with an ordinary household item. Each part of this bird's body is made from a piece of a paper doily. First cut it out carefully, ink it with more than one color, and then print. This approach gives very detailed work.*

Try printing table napkins, lamp shades, and other objects for the home. Always use fabric dyes for material which is to be washed.

## Printing with household objects

Buttons, keys, curtain rings, feathers, paper clips, toothbrushes, matches, balloons, crumpled paper, screws and bolts are just some of the ordinary things which can be used to make prints. On the left is a lovely bird design, printed from parts of a paper doily. Great care was needed when cutting out and printing down.

The problem of holding small objects while printing often arises. Tweezers can be used to hold matchsticks or buttons, but you must have a firm grip or the object may fall on your print. A magnet will hold small metal objects such as keys, keyhole plates and paper clips. Thick adhesive tape stuck over the underside of small objects like curtain rings will hold them steady. When printing with string, first draw your design on a piece of cardboard then glue the string on the design. Cut away the surrounding cardboard, paint the string, and then print it down.

Always use padding underneath the paper when printing with objects like combs or coins. When printing on softer objects like small articles of clothing, cover with folded newspaper, then place a heavy book on top and apply pressure.

## Combined printing and drawing

This is very simple to do, takes the minimum of equipment, and is great fun for children. The animals on page 28 were all carefully printed with potatoes, and then drawn round to give them their full features. Objects used for printing on these two pages were (below, left to right) cotton reels, a cork, buttons, a polystyrene tile, feathers, matches, thick cord, and (above right) a balloon. Ask children to print the same images on sheets of paper and have a competition to see who can make the best drawing around the prints.

Finger and thumb prints combine well with pen and ink drawings, and you can elaborate on them by using crayons, brush, chalk, or fiber-tip pens.

## Things to make

Here are some ideas for things to make, using your prints as a basis for the design.

## Gift wrapping paper

Use colored tissue paper or large sheets of flimsy paper for gift wrappings. A good idea is to print a design that has some connection with the gift to be wrapped. For car enthusiasts, for example, print with spanners (wrenches) or nuts; if the present is connected with sewing or knitting, print with bobbins, scissors or balls of wool. Use a baby's bootee or nappy (diaper) pins for a christening gift, and for wedding presents try curtain rings, interlocked in pairs, or choose a dark tissue paper and print confetti-shaped images in pastel colors.

## Printed paper and envelopes

If the stationery is for you, put your personal motif, such as initials or a flower, on each sheet of paper and print it on each envelope flap too. Either use the motif quite small at the top of the sheet of paper, or let it cover the whole sheet in pale, blending colors. If you are giving sta-

*This balloon was printed with a toy balloon!*

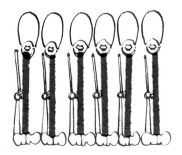

*Drawing has enhanced the prints along the bottom of these two pages.*

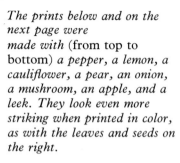

The prints below and on the next page were made with (from top to bottom) *a pepper, a lemon, a cauliflower, a pear, an onion, a mushroom, an apple, and a leek. They look even more striking when printed in color, as with the leaves and seeds on the right.*

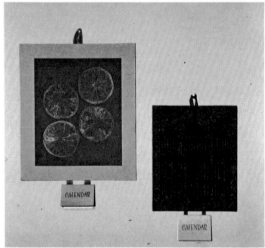

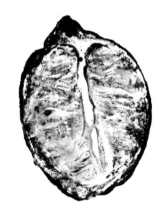

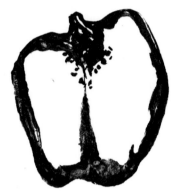

tionery as a gift and buy it ready-boxed, cover the lid with material of similar design to the writing paper.

### Greetings cards

It's economical to make Christmas and birthday or all-purpose cards all together for use throughout the year. Buy inexpensive envelopes and cut cards to fit them. Fold the cards once if using thin card (pasteboard) or twice if using cartridge (drawing) paper.

Combined printing and drawing is effective for humorous cards: a handwritten greeting will make the card all the more personal.

### Calendars

The large calendar above was made by printing grapefruit halves on brown cardboard and framing it with lemon-colored paper.

The smaller calendar was made with a piece of card (pasteboard) covered in plain fabric which was then printed with cardboard and matches, dipped in printing ink.

### Wall-hangings

Hem a piece of material top and bottom, slide a piece of beading inside each hem, and print a design on the fabric. Material that frays easily should also be hemmed at the sides or stabilized with fabric adhesive. The material used for the wall-hanging above was a piece of dyed cellular blanket, printed with cardboard and poster paints.

### Table napkins

Use oil-based inks for printing on paper

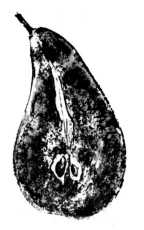

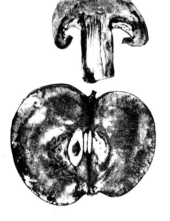

napkins, but, as they will be thrown away after use, don't spend too long on an elaborate design.

Make cloth napkins by cutting and hemming 300 mm (12 in.) squares, and print on them with fabric dyes. If you want an unusual effect, instead of hemming, fringe the napkins by pulling several strands of fabric away from the raw edges.

*Printing with fruit and vegetables*
Use the basic equipment needed for potato printing, and experiment with other vegetables and fruit. Carrots, swedes (rutabagas), parsnips and turnips are all solid and as easy to cut and print with as potatoes. Apples, pears, cauliflowers and peppers are softer but still fairly easy to work with. Pomegranates, onions, citrus fruits and tomatoes are very soft and, after cutting, need to be left to dry out and harden for some time before printing.

Fruit pips, stones and skins can also be used. If using a very small object, attach a handle made from a strip of adhesive tape. For cabbage and other large leaves, use padding underneath the paper on which you are printing. Fruit and vegetable prints are shown on the left.

*Printing from nature*
Prints can be made from any natural object: ferns, fine twigs, bark, fir cones, berries, nuts, seeds, small stones, grasses. Flat objects like leaves and grasses will give a better print if you use padding. To make a bark print, choose a fairly thin piece and stick adhesive tape over the underside to act as a backing. Flatten the bark gently but firmly, and when printing use plenty of padding, cover the bark with folded newspaper, and apply pressure with your fingers.

On the right are examples of bark, ivy, fern, sycamore seeds, seeding rosebay willow herb, sand dune grass, chestnut husk, buttercup leaf and bramble leaf.

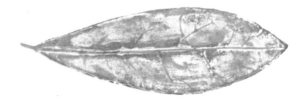

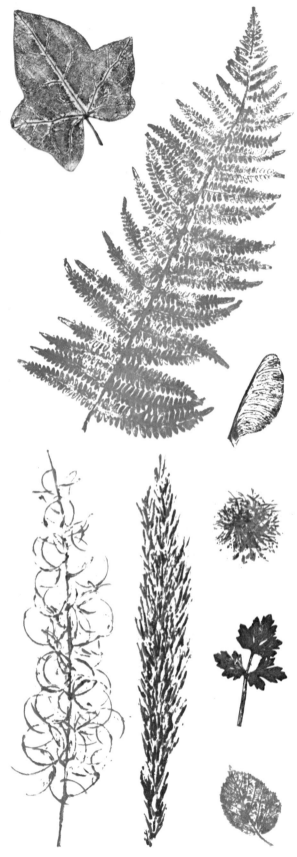

# A Leaf Zoo

Many people, even children (who ought to know better) are under the impression that they cannot draw, paint or produce works of art of any kind. They are mistaken. It is just that the way in which they are able to show their artistic creativity is outside the conventional idea of 'art'. Some of these supposedly amateur, untrained artists have made extraordinarily exciting objects or pictures that have justly earned the approval of art experts.

This chapter shows a series of such works, made entirely from leaves, which it is hoped will inspire you to make a zoo of your own imaginative and haunting creatures. They can be given to friends, used to decorate walls or objects, made into greetings cards, or just kept for your own pleasure.

Once you try designs of this kind, you will soon find how easy it is to produce amusing and

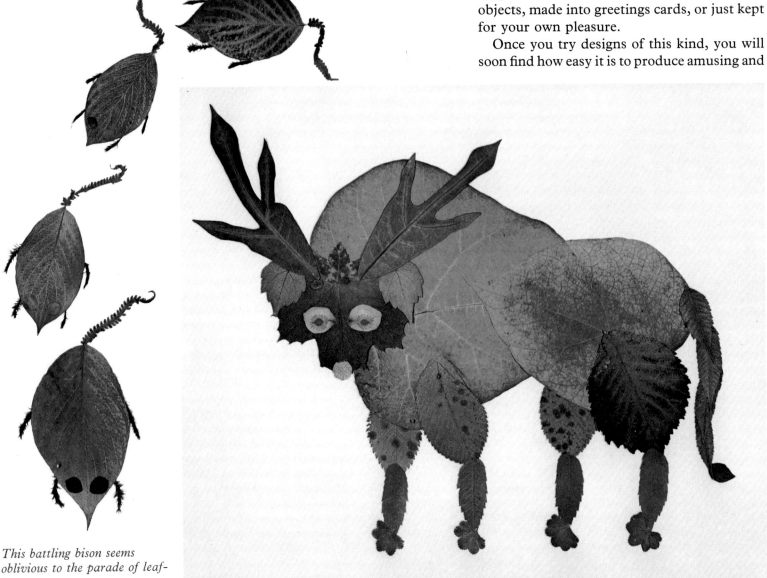

*This battling bison seems oblivious to the parade of leaflets.*

*A spiny lobster prepares to attack a sad, multi-colored fish.*

often beautiful things from natural materials.

*Starting to make pictures*
Making leaf creatures is an amusing occupation for everyone, adults as well as children, and especially for those who have to spend long hours tied to an office or to a school desk. There is something exhilarating about being able to give free rein to your imagination in creating these fantasy creatures, and even the untrained eye will soon begin to spot the creative possibilities of a handful of varied leaves. The best place to work is on the floor, as you will need a lot of room to spread out all your materials. Don't start with a preconceived idea of what the animal is going to look like at the end. You can of course, just copy the models illustrated here, but, as you go along, you will want to add or subtract here and there to produce your own inventions.

Collect leaves wherever you go. Press them between the pages of telephone directories or other large books with no precious pages that might be spoiled, as leaves can stain the paper and ruin valuable books. Telephone directories

35

*A sad, obedient, geranium-eared, straw-tailed stumpmouse.*

*A browny-green jolly-hopper and a Zanzibar rat.*

are the best for pressing, not only because they are heavy, and you don't have to worry about spoiling or staining them, but also because they have an alphabetical listing. This means you can slip beetles into B pages, squirrels into S, and so on. Or you can arrange leaves according to tree or plant, or by color.

Press leaves as soon as possible after collection. Don't leave them in a heated room for more than half an hour or they will curl up and eventually crumble, which is a great waste of time.

You will find that some leaves behave strangely when pressed. For instance, wine-red autumn leaves don't like too heavy a weight; if you press them too hard, they will turn black. This can also happen with some fresh spring leaves.

Collect lime, chestnut, horse chestnut, willow and any other leaves with good shapes. Store them carefully and, when they are well pressed, take them out, scatter them on the floor and see what kinds of creatures emerge from random grouping.

36

As you are not going to paint the leaves, you can arrange them in piles according to color, size and shape, as if they were so many pots of paint and as if the floor were one large palette. Get to know the leaves as you would a range of painting colors.

## Tools and materials

All you need in the way of materials, apart from lots of leaves of all shapes and sizes, is card (pasteboard) or cartridge (drawing) paper for mounting them and an acid-free adhesive for gluing them. Ask your crafts supplier about which to buy. Apart from this, all you need is imagination, patience and the enthusiasm of the collector!

## Starting work

Don't let the dog or cat into the room where you are laying out your leaves, and don't open the windows or the wind will blow your designs about. On the other hand, if it does, leaves are easily come by and you may find an even better pattern when you come to rearrange them.

*A rusty, rumbustious frog-snapper meets his match.*

*A finely-detailed lambling.*

There is no need to make any preliminary sketch or design for your leaf creatures. Ideas will come from the variety of leaves you have collected. They will be sparked off either by the shape of one leaf or the shape made by two or more leaves placed together. Inspiration can also come from a mixture of leaf colors. As in a painting, if you put a walnut green next to a tobacco brown, suddenly a new life can come into being, suggesting its own form and character.

Animals can be combined in a leaf zoo. You can have a goose with a cat's face, or forget the goose and settle for an Egyptian cat. An orchid can suddenly turn into a Chinese carp and an oak leaf into a stag's antlers.

Animals can change half-way through as well. Butterflies look just as fine if you change

*A leaf-fox has stumbled on a strange creature in the forest. Is it fish or is it fowl?*

them into squirrels or lizards. Fish can take to the air on mysterious and exotic wings. Birds are always a favorite subject. They can be proud, humble, long-legged, small and cheerful or haughty and ridiculous (see those on this page for a few ideas). You can give them giraffe heads and necks, or make them creep along the ground or blow themselves up like frogs. Perhaps birds are most successful because

autumn leaf colors are close to those of natural feathers.

Leaves and dried and pressed flowers go well together in a leaf picture. Forsythia and blackberry, wild rose and rhododendron, apple and cress, cultivated and wild, from park or hedgerow, are some of the many varieties of flowers you can try mixing with leaves.

One danger with these leaf pictures is that the colors fade very quickly in strong sunlight and fade gradually in ordinary daylight. The best way to preserve color is to keep the greater part of the collection pasted on sheets of sugar

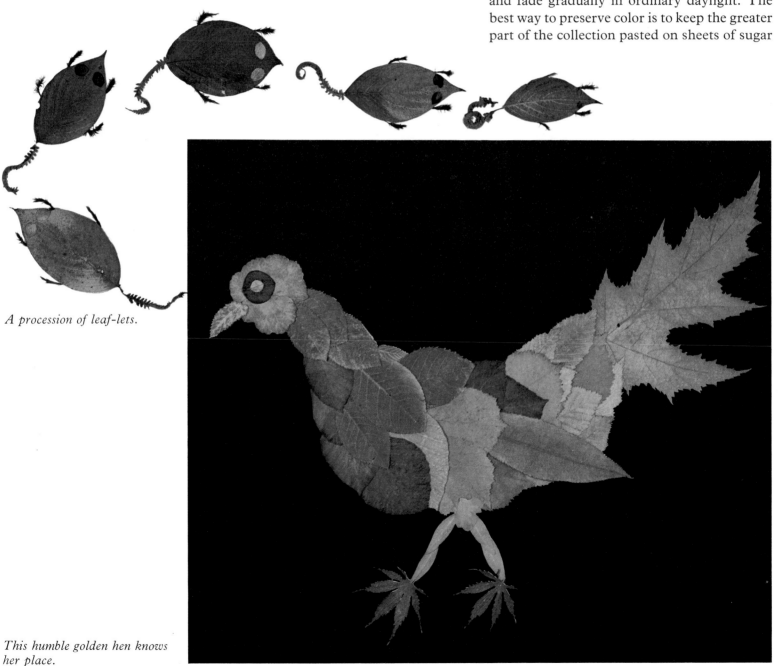

*A procession of leaf-lets.*

*This humble golden hen knows her place.*

*Ostrich feathers have many of the qualities of the pot plants once found in halls and reception areas. They have long, loose bracts which drift with a slight movement of the surrounding air. This ostrich plant was made by wiring a number of these feathers to wire stems, and then assembling them in a tub of florist's foam to hold them firm.*

# Feather Flowers

The Victorians, with their passion for craftwork, were quick to realize that the varied and subtle qualities of birds' plumage made it an attractive material for decorative purposes. Many museums contain examples of their work in the form of feather flowers, usually placed under a glass dome to protect them from wear and tear.

Today the pleasure of making feather flower arrangements is being rediscovered. The same raw materials, so generously supplied by nature, are used, but techniques have improved, as have ideas on color and design.

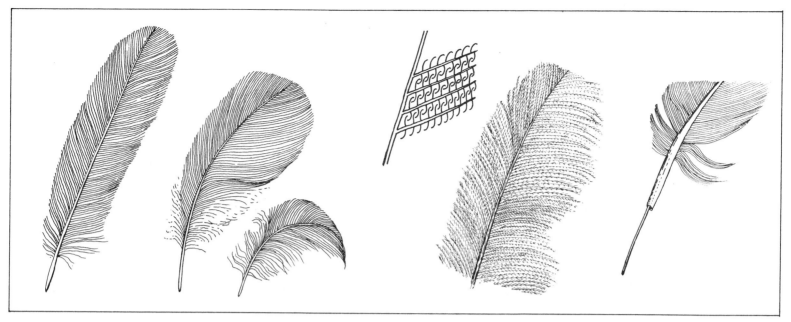

## What feathers to use

It must be emphasized that feathercraft uses only *discarded* feathers and that, however enthusiastic you become, no harm must ever be done to living birds.

There are two main types of feather: the stiff flight feathers, and the contour feathers, which fit the contours of the body closely, and tend to be fluffy for warmth. Only tail and crest feathers are really straight; wing feathers curve slightly according to which side of the bird they come from. Both straight and curved flight feathers are suitable for making leaf shapes. The softer body feathers, which also curve, can be used as petals.

## Where to get feathers

Many crafts shops sell feathers ready-dyed. Zoo and bird-park keepers will often let you have (or buy) cast-off feathers from their exotic inmates. Local rummage sales and junk shops sometimes have feather dusters or old feather-decorated garments, and local farmers or poultry shops are often glad to be rid of their surplus poultry feathers.

Goose, chicken and turkey feathers are all good for craftwork. They are strong, plain and dye very well. Guinea fowl, partridge, mallard and teal all have patterns which can be made use of, while the peacock, golden pheasant and ring-neck pheasant have beautifully patterned plumage. Even more lovely are the Lady Amherst and Reeves Silver pheasants. All these, of course, are only examples. If feathers from none of these birds are available locally, you are sure to be able to find others that are equally effective. If you are lucky enough to get hold of rare feathers, be sure that they are well displayed in your design.

## Tools and materials

Feathers, glue, hot water dyes, wires, stem binding material (obtainable from florists) and materials for flower centers are the main requirements for feather flowers. You will also need sharp scissors, wire cutters, pins and a knife.

## Cutting feathers

Feathers are wonderful examples of natural design. Each one is composed of rows of tiny feathers, each in turn connected to a central vein. Every tiny feather or bract has a row of hooks on either side that interlocks with the row next to it to make the feather smooth. When the hooks remain separate, the feather is fluffy. The central vein is hollow and can be used to advantage when you want to insert a wire into a feather.

When cutting feathers, always use very sharp scissors, for feathers are surprisingly tough and springy. First decide on your shape, then cut

*The feathers in the drawing are* (from left to right): *an almost straight tail feather; a back and a breast feather compared; interlocking hooks on a feather bract; non-interlocking hooks with a fluffy effect; and a wire inserted into a cut-off feather-end.*

43

the whole side of a feather in one slice with large, sharp scissors. Little snips usually result in a ragged looking feather. When making leaves or petals, vary the points slightly. A thinner point is elegant on a leaf, but petals should be cut to be more rounded. When choosing feathers, use only the best. Poor ones make inferior flowers.

Trimming is one way of removing surplus feather. You can strip individual bracts from a central vein and, in the case of large feathers like peacock, save the bracts for further use. When making a leaf, once you have shaped the top of the feather, you can strip away the lower part to leave a realistic shape standing on its own stem. A bunch of these made from tiny feathers can be assembled and used to make the protruding stamens of pendant flowers such as fuchsias.

## Curving

All feathers have a natural curve but you can add more if you like. Some feathers will curve more easily than others: when curving, it is best to use flat feathers with soft center veins, like those known as 'sattins', from the underside of

*A beautifully-colored basket of fluffies. The big flowers are made from goose nagoire shoulder feathers filled out in the center with marabou. Other flowers are made from ostrich feathers and white turkey feathers. As all these are very fluffy, a few dark lilies made from curled goose sattin wing feathers have been added for contrast.*

*This drawing shows you how to shape the top of a feather to give a leaf effect. It also shows how to strip away the lower part so that you have a realistic shape standing on its own stem.*

the wing. Holding the feather on the blade with your thumb, use a blunt knife or closed pair of scissors to squeeze the vein along its length until you get the required curve. This is shown in the drawing below. Do not pull the feather or you may destroy its contour, which must remain intact. Repeat the process gently until you have enough curve. If the bracts separate, coax them back together by pulling so that little hooks re-engage: a simple movement like that made by birds with their beaks.

## Coloring

Feathers are easily dyed with hot water fabric dye; follow the instructions on the packet carefully. It is important to boil the feathers because this breaks down their water resistance, which varies in strength according to whether they came from land or water birds. Once you are satisfied that they have absorbed all the dye, place the feathers on a pad of newspaper in front of a fan heater or hair dryer and blow them dry. This should restore the fluff, but if you are not satisfied, hold the feather in steam (be careful!) for half a minute. If you have a lot of feathers to steam, bring a preserving pan of water to the boil and place the feathers on a wire cake rack over this. Don't stroke the feathers until they are fully dry, as if you do you will flatten the hooks and have to begin again.

## Making centers

The center, the focal point around which the feather petals are wrapped to encase the seed, is a very important part of the flower. Generally, however small, it should be prominent and easily recognizable. But there are exceptions to this rule, for flowers such as roses or carnations have too many petals for the center to be visible. So when you are imitating flowers like these, make the center out of a material that blends with the petals of the flower. Small whole dried flowers are suitable as centers.

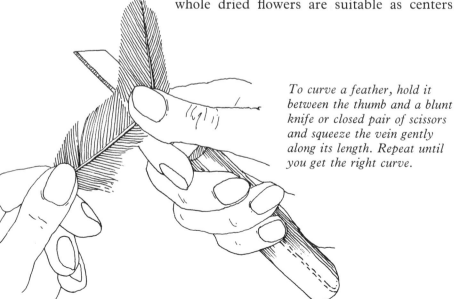

*To curve a feather, hold it between the thumb and a blunt knife or closed pair of scissors and squeeze the vein gently along its length. Repeat until you get the right curve.*

Bind a bunch very tightly to the top of a stem wire with binding wire before adding petals. You can even use a fir cone as a holder for feather petals: choose one similar in size to the petals you are to use. The cone will probably have lost its stem, so hook over the top of the stem wire and insert it between the lower scales of the cone.

You can use flowers as centers. Make a bunch of peacock or ostrich feather bracts, curling them so that the resulting spirals tumble outwards over the petals. A fluffy center contrasts well with flat, shiny feathers. If you find one or two special feathers, use them as a center, with appropriate petals to go with them. Small shiny beads form a perfect contrast to soft feathers, and can be massed on their own wire stems so they stand above the fluff at the base of the feathers. Pearls are perfect centers for white wedding flowers, and gold or silver centers look festive at Christmas.

*Gluing flowers*
When using a fir cone center, apply clear glue carefully between the scales and push the feathers right in. Assemble the petals first,

*You can make a feather flower center from a tiny cluster of whole dried flowers bound tightly to the top of the stem wire. You can do this even more effectively with curled peacock or ostrich feather bracts (see below).*

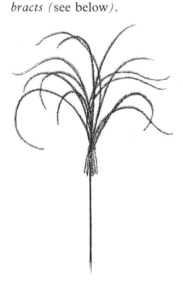

*This peacock flower arrangement was assembled on a piece of olive wood. Use back feathers in a curved line for the flowers. Make the blue flowers from feathers that grow further down the bird's back, and the tumbling stamens from the side of the tail feathers.*

*A peacock's fan reassembled from feathers lost during moulting.*

*You can fill the entire center of a lily with a single marabou feather.*

cutting the ends even, before applying the glue, as it dries very rapidly. Teazels also have scales which will hold feathers. Because of their shape and size, these need large, flat feathers.

Florist's foam can form a center core into which feathers can be pushed. This is usually bought ready-shaped, but if you have a melon ball cutter you can cut your own shapes from a larger piece. Dip the bases of the feathers in glue and, starting at the top center of the ball, push them into it until it is covered. Tiny feathers can be used in this way to make a small rose.

Large foam spheres are readily obtainable. As a whole sphere is usually too big for most flowers, cut one in half. So that you can keep the feathers level while you are assembling the flower, work with the foam flat on the table and add the stem afterwards. When you are ready to add the stem, twine three wires together, leaving 25 mm (1 in.) fanned out at the top, and cover all but the tips with green stem binding material. Glue these three tips to the back of the flower to support the heavy head. Glue feathers to any foam that is still visible.

Another method is to fill a center with small

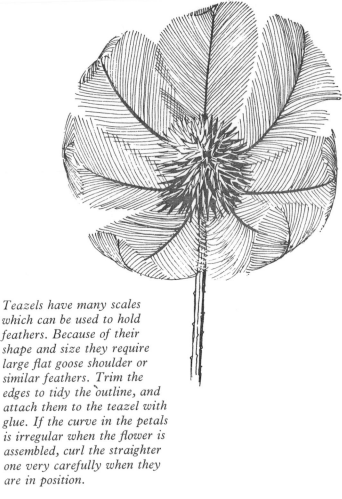

Teazels have many scales which can be used to hold feathers. Because of their shape and size they require large flat goose shoulder or similar feathers. Trim the edges to tidy the outline, and attach them to the teazel with glue. If the curve in the petals is irregular when the flower is assembled, curl the straighter one very carefully when they are in position.

*This soft array of delicate little flowers was inspired by allium heads. Each feather flower was assembled into a ball and attached to a stem. There is a small piece of marabou at the center of each of them. This arrangement should last three years at least.*

dried flowers, then bind the petals to the stem.

### Assembling flowers

Flowers can be assembled with wire instead of glue. Use a very fine wire for binding and a much heavier straight wire for the stem. To prevent the flower collapsing, bind each feather as tightly as possible to the stem. When binding, hold the feather firmly in position and don't let it rotate with the binding. Keep the same piece of wire throughout the assembly and try to avoid excessive binding, as this creates a bulky joint below the petals. Thin

feathers tend to twist, so put several on at once and then they will hold each other straight.

Mixed flower arrangements must include some blooms with a good profile. Many hand-made flowers are round, so to vary the shapes try bending some to point downwards, and add a bunch of pendant stamens. A fuchsia, for example, has two layers of petals with stamens, and the final layer should curl back sufficiently to allow the rest of the flower to be visible. Exotic lilies can be imitated in feathers. Use flat wing sattins and curl them until you have enough petals to assemble.

*A globe-shaped flower-head consisting of tiny curly duck or teal breast feathers is a very realistic imitation of a rose on the point of blooming.*

*Bind feather leaves on alternate sides of a stem during stem binding. You do not need any bulky additional wire.*

*A dome of flowers from a ring-necked pheasant. It is designed as a dining-table centerpiece and is built on a candlestick. The white feather leaves were added to hide the less attractive flower-stems.*

When designing flowers, remember that the number of petals should be the same as, or a multiple of, the number of stamens in the center.

*Leaves*

Few flower arrangements are complete without leaves. Single feathers from exotic birds such as macaws, peacocks, flamingos and pheasants can make an imposing addition to an arrangement, either whole or with parts stripped from the center vein.

Some ostrich and peacock feathers have long, separate bracts which can be curled all the way up for variety. Pheasant tail feathers can look a little severe, but if you strip one side and curl the whole length, they add big swirling lines to a cluster of flowers.

If you have only small feathers to work with, you can assemble them on wire stems to form sprays of leaves. No extra binding wire is necessary for these sprays; all you have to do is simply join each leaf during the stem binding process. Arranged on alternate sides of the spray, these leaves look very realistic and add variety to a feather flower arrangement.

# Seed Decorations

Most seeds are attractive in shape and color, and when they are placed together or combined in types, they offer a wide range of patterns and shapes. This makes working with seeds an excellent craft for those without much artistic confidence. Even the simplest stripes, chevrons and circles often make very effective patterns, yet they demand no great creative talent.

Seeds cost little or nothing, the other equipment needed is minimal, and containers to be decorated are easy to find. Seed decorations last for years, though their colors may

*A framed picture using a wide variety of colorful seeds.*

*This candleholder started life as a talcum-powder can. It was already colored. Therefore seeds that would blend in with these colors were used: wheat, yellow split peas and black rape.*

*A generous arrangement of seed flowers made as described on page 57.*

*This can had a good airtight seal. After decoration with rice, natural lentils, millet and tares it could be used for storing tea.*

change.slightly. But look out for mice! They like seeds and have absolutely no respect for creativity at all.

*Finding seeds*
Autumn is the best time to start collecting all seeds. Hang up to dry all flower or vegetable seed heads that have either a good shape or interesting contents. Poppy heads are nearly always attractive in shape and grow in many sizes. The seeds inside honesty are pretty, and it's worth going to the trouble to get them out. On country walks, collect as much material as you can, such as fir cones, acorns and their cups, sycamore and ash wings, and pieces from the spiky branches of the monkey puzzle tree. These are just a few suggestions. You will find that the possibilities are almost endless.

Other sources of seeds are corn or seed merchants, large pet shops or animal feed suppliers and wholefood shops. You should be able to find wheat, groats, maple peas, white and striped sunflower seeds, black and red rape (used as bird food), paddy rice, tares, milo (sorghum), black eye beans and millet. From foreign and health food shops you can buy

*This rook shows how you can use the general shape and color of an animal to make a very lively design.*

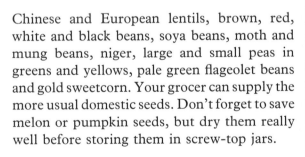

*A sun design worked on a specially-prepared batik backing. The linen backing was then mounted on board to give a firm base to work on.*

to decorate a cigar box to hold the odds and ends you need for working with seeds.

*Glue.* This is the first essential material. PVA is an excellent adhesive and it is found on sale in art and crafts suppliers and Do-It-Yourself shops. The great advantage of this glue is that when dry it is clear, colorless, invisible and very strong. When mixed with water in a solution of one part adhesive to two parts water, it can be used as a protective varnish for the finished work. Always squeeze glue out a little at a time, and replace the top as PVA dries out quickly. If it is in a jar, it is even more important to replace the top.

*Craft knife.* One with a replaceable blade is very useful for splitting and for trimming the seeds.

*Toothpicks.* Those that are pointed at one end and flat at the other are the most useful as they help to put the glue exactly where you want it and can also help to pick up the smallest seeds.

Chinese and European lentils, brown, red, white and black beans, soya beans, moth and mung beans, niger, large and small peas in greens and yellows, pale green flageolet beans and gold sweetcorn. Your grocer can supply the more usual domestic seeds. Don't forget to save melon or pumpkin seeds, but dry them really well before storing them in screw-top jars.

*Tools and materials*

Most of the tools you need will probably be in your home already. Gather them all together before you start work and try to provide a spare surface where you can leave your work between sessions. An appropriate first exercise would be

*An arrogant cockerel made from sunflower seeds, kidney beans, sweetcorn, marrow seeds, corn and many other seeds.*

*A very detailed design in seeds is hard to produce unless it is very large. This house shows how you can use seeds to suggest the textures of surfaces and objects. Keep the shapes simple. Natural lentils form the roof, and tares the walls. The trees are moth, mung and flageolet beans and yellow lentil apples. In the garden are wheat, split peas and bits of cane and the chimney smoke is made of linseeds.*

friends know you are on the look-out for unusual cardboard cylinders, empty cigar boxes or interesting bottles, you will soon build up a good store. Tobacconists will sometimes let you have empty cigar boxes for a small sum of money.

*Strong cardboard.* This is needed to back pictures and to use for frames. Strawboard (matboard) serves most purposes and can be bought by the sheet in art and crafts shops.

*Other items.* A pencil, a ruler, a pair of scissors, elastic bands and cheap white paper will all come in useful.

### Fabric and other backings

Many of the objects illustrated in this chapter were painted or covered with fabric before the seeds were applied, and all the pictures were worked on fabric-covered backings.

The choice of fabric is important as it must match in with the seeds and not distract from them. In most cases, plain natural earthy colors are more suitable than very bright ones, so choose white, cream, beige, brown, black, ocher, burnt orange, moss green or gray-blue. All of these colors are close to those of the earth and are more likely to harmonize with seeds. However, sometimes bright colors can be appropriate. Cylinders and boxes covered with scarlet felt or paper and decorated with black

For spreading larger areas of adhesive, cut some rectangles of strong cardboard, about 25 × 50 mm (1 × 2 in.), and use these to spread the adhesive.

*Tweezers.* Used to pick up and position seeds which are too small to handle with your fingers.

*Varnish.* A tin of clear polyurethane varnish and a small paint brush will be needed when it comes to the varnishing stage.

*Containers.* Use objects that you have about the house, such as bottles, pill bottles, cardboard boxes, sweet (candy) boxes and old cans. All of these you would normally discard as rubbish, but they can be used in seed work and will look completely different when decorated. Once

and white seeds make splendid Christmas gifts, for example.

Felt is a good material for covering containers, as it can easily be cut to any shape and needs no hemming. It is made in a wide range of lovely colors too. Hessians (burlaps) are also suitable and they come in pleasant natural colors with a simple woven texture of variable coarseness. Consider the size of the seeds you intend to use when choosing your backing fabric. Coarse fabrics are suitable for large seeds, smoother ones for smaller, more delicate seeds. On the right is a diagram of how to turn down fabric over board to make a smooth corner.

*How to work*

Before attempting your first pictures or anything more than the simplest pattern, take a piece of cardboard or perhaps a rectangular cork mat and experiment with seed designs on it for a while. Start with the middle-sized and larger seeds and arrange them in strips of different widths and simple groups until you begin to get the knack of handling them. When you have an arrangement you like, fix them

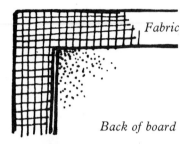

*Fabric*

*Back of board*

*Fabric turned and stuck to the back of the board*

*Spare fabric flattened and stuck down*

These three candleholders were made from strong cardboard cones that once held weaving thread. Each was decorated with leaves and seeds, including monkey puzzle spines, tares, maple peas, European lentils and even petals from globe artichokes.

54

*Make these Christmas tree decorations with cardboard disks as bases on which you glue seeds and beans. For the method, follow the instructions for making flowers on page 57.*

with the glue. You will soon find which shapes and colors combine well together and how much adhesive you need to glue them. Then perhaps you can try a circular pattern, starting from a central seed and working outwards.

When you have had more practice, you will probably want to try a more elaborate design. To get a basic design shape, try folding and cutting a piece of paper. Cut boldly but simply into the folded paper and then open it out to see the total design. Make as many attempts as you need until you arrive at a shape you like, then interpret this shape in seeds. You can work out

the pattern with loose seeds on a piece of felt or set the seeds lightly into a sheet of non-hardening modeling clay and then copy the design on its permanent background.

When sticking the seeds down, use the end of a toothpick to apply the adhesive over the small areas of the background, and place the larger seeds one at a time with your fingers or tweezers. For larger shapes built up from a number of very small seeds, make the shape in glue first, then sprinkle it with the seeds, pushing them close together. A tiny spot of glue on the end of a toothpick will make it possible to

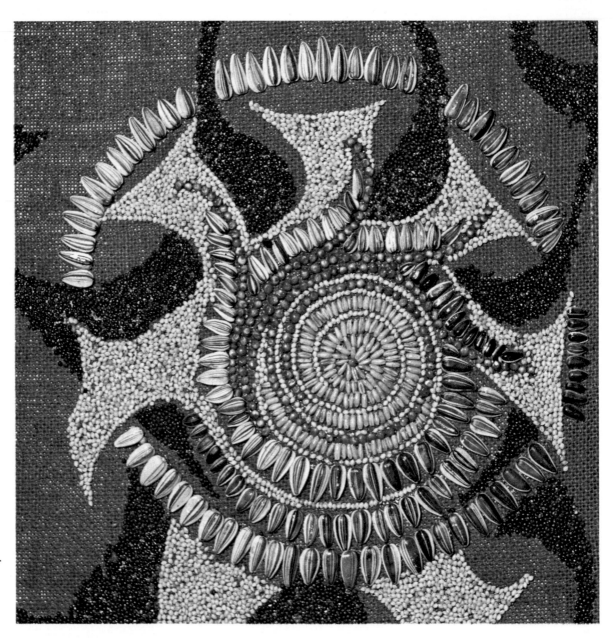

*Abstract designs offer freedom to the designer. This one was worked on a background of hessian (burlap) stretched over a board until taut. A single seed was placed in the center and the design spiraled out from there.*

pick up a single small seed. If you give the end of the toothpick a lick and then dip it into a pile of small seeds, you will be able to pick up about a dozen at a time, and place them on a ready-glued surface.

*Painting and varnishing*
Any gloss paint is suitable for painting cans and jars before seed decoration. If you intend to varnish the finished work, then it is best to use emulsion paint. Always remember that two thin coats of paint are better than one thick coat, which may run or wrinkle.

Varnishing serves several purposes. The varnish increases the richness of color of the seeds and protects them from dust. It also protects them from some damage, though it will not save them from hard knocks. Varnish keeps the small seeds more securely in place, as once varnished they are not only glued from underneath but are also covered by a thin adhesive glaze of varnish on top. If glossy varnish is too shiny, then use a matt or eggshell finish varnish.

Where the design is backed with fabric or glass, the varnish must be brushed on very carefully with a small brush to avoid touching the background. Spray varnish can be used on painted backgrounds. An alternative is to use a solution of PVA adhesive and water as a protective covering over seeds, fabric or cork. When it dries it is invisible and has a slight glaze.

*Covering boxes*
The main point to remember when covering all boxes and containers which are handled or opened frequently is to leave undecorated the parts that meet each other. For example, seeds stuck all over the back of a box, tight up to the hinges, will be crushed when the box is opened! An elastic band slipped round the box below the hinges will give you a guide as to how far you can decorate when making a band of seeds.

*Flowers*
A vase of seed flowers can look very pretty and need not be too difficult to make. As a base on which to construct the seed 'petals', use a large button or a circle of strong cardboard, through which has first been threaded a strong flower wire which will act as a stem. Bind the stem with green binding material such as florist's tape, or with strips of green or brown crêpe paper wound tightly round the wire.

Start on the outside of the button or cardboard and stick on a layer of 'petals'. Work towards the center with circles of different colored and shaped seeds.

This method has been used for the Christmas decorations on page 55.

*Pictures*
Seed pictures can be designed directly on different kinds of cork, wooden panels, felt or fabric.

Covering a piece of strawboard (matboard) with the fabric you have chosen is a simple operation. Cut the board to the required size, then cut the fabric about 40 mm (1½ in.) wider all round. Fold the corners over (following the diagram on page 54) as you glue the overhanging fabric to the back of the board. Pull the fabric tightly across the front of the board as you glue so that you have a firm, taut surface to work on.

You may find it difficult to think of subjects for your design. Photographs of birds, fish and insects are useful starting points for designs. It is best not to try to be too realistic though, so don't make a very detailed copy of the creature you use, but base your design on the *general* shape and color only.

Abstracts are excellent subjects for seed pictures. The one on the opposite page has been done on a hessian (burlap) background, and the design started with a single seed placed right at the center, with the rest of the design spiraling out from that point.

Lamp bases, mirror frames, cork notepads, kitchen jars and plant pots, even cupboard doors, are some of the many things which can successfully be decorated with seeds.

*A wall design worked on cork.*

*Two specimens of garden cuckoo-pint* (Arum italicum) *are the central attractions of this superb little display. Arrange it in an antique brass scoop containing a bed of moss peat. Include chrysanthemums, rose hips, elderberries and hops* (Humulus eupulus). *During the summer months, African marigolds or gillyflowers* (Tagetes erecta) *and red-hot pokers* (Kniphofia) *are striking alternative additions.*

# Flower Arrangements

Flowers are so lovely in themselves that if you had enough money simply to buy as many as you wanted, little artistic skill would be needed to arrange them. Their colors and their magnificence in quantity would speak for themselves. But few of us can afford to do this. However, there can be great pleasure and satisfaction in the craft of choosing and displaying a *few* available flowers. Those who know how to show off a flower can display a single dahlia or rose so that it has as much impact as ten or twenty of them. And what could be a more delightful symbol of the arrival of spring than a tiny spray of daisies or wood violets?

In arranging just a few flowers, every element is important. Consider the effect that the arrangement will have on a room as a whole. Choose the right accompaniments, such as appropriately shaped and colored vases, impressive sprays or branches of greenery, twigs, or branches or wood bark to act as backgrounds. You can make other additions, such as fruit, vegetables, gourds or fir or pine cones, all of which increase the impact of flowers by making them the brilliant center of a total arrangement. In this way you can increase the decorative effect of even the smallest bunch of flowers.

Here are some basic arrangements from which you can develop your own variations.

Remember the golden rule: that major successes are most often achieved by small and subtle means!

*Vases*

When making your collection of vases and containers, there are some important points to consider. The vases should either be of a type to show off the form and detail of the flowers you have, or they should be so striking in shape or color that they become an essential part of the composition.

To start with, look at bottles, water jugs, decanters and carafes, all of which have narrow necks or small openings (see the picture below). You don't have to build up a collection of valuable antique bottles either, since many drinks come in inexpensive but attractive

*Narrow-necked bottles make fine display bases: in this example, the richly-tinted zinnias are set off by the background of* Rosa rubrifolia, *held tight in the bottle.*

*A round, squat vase of this type is a solid and stable base for a tall and wavering display. The purple flower here is clary* (Salvia sclarea) *and the greenery is hops.*

containers which might normally be thrown away. Look in your kitchen cupboards; there are sure to be some suitable jars and bottles there already. Try using a number of bottles and jars of contrasting shapes: one with spring greenery, perhaps, one with a few daffodils, another with wood violets, ragwort or spruce.

Now have a long look at stemmed glasses, goblets or containers which give an arrangement additional height and allow the flowers to spread out elegantly above a slender or unusually shaped stalk. Sometimes other decorative objects can be incorporated. A copper

or brass scoop (see page 58) a fine old tea caddy (see page 63), a box or a sea shell can do much to bring out the quality and color of flowers.

*Flower supports*
Open-necked vessels such as dishes and goblets can be used for variegated displays. The stems of flowers need to be put into a bed of supporting material, such as florist's foam. All sorts of flower embedding materials can be bought from local florists; some can be molded to the required shape, others have to be cut.

Sometimes the material has to be soaked first, for it is difficult to stick stems into a dry, hard base. A useful aid is green binding thread, used for binding the ends of stems to make insertion into the foam easier.

To support flowers, you can also use wire netting, peat moss, lead-based wire supports in beds of moss under a layer of gravel, glass marbles or marble chips.

To make a small arrangement against the side of a glass dish, a support wire can be passed through a small ball of plastic or non-hardening modeling clay, and the plant fixed to it.

*What to use for foliage*

You can usually get sprigs of fir, pine, spruce, or similar from even the most conventional florist, and they make ideal settings for flower displays. Use material like this to fill your vase, dish or bowl before you begin the subtle and individual work of trying out different flowers in varying combinations against a set background. It is usually most effective if you cut the background material to about 25 mm (1 in.) above the rim of the container, so that it does not dominate in color, or interfere with the display of the flowers being used.

*A small candle makes a high point for this simple winter arrangement.*

However, in more unusual arrangements with only a few flowers, sprigs from the rich, dark firs, pines, larches and spruces can play an effective part. Use them as equals to the flowers. If the neck of a jug, bottle or decanter, for instance, is too wide for the flowers, then start off with some sprigs of fir which will fill the opening and allow the main blooms to be positioned just where they are required. You can use sprigs and branches from other trees too, though conifers do last longest, on the whole. If you want to keep green material for a while, store it in a cool place in a bucket containing a little water.

Some other suitable green plants are *Mahonia aquifolium*, with its striking looking brown, burnished leaves, the evergreen holly, and the green parts of the rhododendron and the *Aucuba japonica*. In winter, when green foliage is scarce, cabbage (kale) makes a good display. Don't forget that herbs such as parsley make decorative foliage, as do many so-called weeds. Sorrel has excellent leaves, and the deep green leaves of cow parsley (wild chervil) are lovely in shape as well as color

### Group displays

If you want a small flower arrangement to develop into or form part of a more sophisticated display, it can be included in a group of other decorative items. The eye is then attracted not only by the flowers but also by the texture and balance of the whole composition. Attractive extras are objects such as gourds, pine cones, a bowl or basket of fruit or even large, interesting stones. It can be pleasing to have a large-stemmed bowl filled with a mixture of flowers and other objects. When the flowers' stalks have to be kept in water, a wire netting support can be placed over the water, allowing the stems to pass through it while the

*The wine glass (above left) is packed with a piece of foam rubber or sponge to support the plants. They are: two dahlias, some Acidanthera bicolor, a spray of elderberries and bunches of green grapes.*

*These short-stemmed chrysanthemums (above right) are accompanied by a few extra sprigs. The pink is echoed in the carnation (Dianthus) and Protea enhances the effect. The contrasting colors are provided by Cedris atlantica glauca and hanging pods of Decaisnea fargesii.*

heavier objects are protected from the water by the wire net. Shaped tree stumps or pieces of driftwood make decorative accompaniments to flowers, and can also serve to hold plants in their nooks and crannies. Thistles often go well with such pieces. Combinations of flowers and other objects can be varied. The glass of grapes on the opposite page, for instance, will become appropriate to spring if the elderberries are replaced with two types of lilac and the dahlias with hyacinths, iris or azaleas. In summer, replace the elderberries with lady's mantle and select as large flowers a few roses, allium or African marigolds.

In the picture above left, the rich tone of the meadow saffron harmonizes perfectly with the groups of glassware against which the small flower display is positioned. This is an arrangement which will provide a great deal of pleasure. The goblet holds a piece of moist bedding material, into which is mounted a bright pelargonium, treated so as to allow it to be replanted later into a plant pot. Heather has been inserted here and there into the bedding, and so has some meadow saffron. This arrangement needs a lot of water if the plants are to remain alive and well.

### Mixing the tones

Making bouquets in different tones of the same color can be interesting and quite challenging. On the previous page is an illustration of an arrangement in different shades of pink, but you could also repeat this theme in tones of blue, or in yellows and oranges. Instead of a pink chrysanthemum, for example, you could use blue scabious (daisy fleabane) with different sorts of campanula and blue-colored thistles, or *Echinops ritro* and/or *Eryngium hybridum*. Blue hortensia, bunches of forget-me-nots, campanulas or veronica can also be

*The ceramic goblet* (above left) *contains an unusual design of small pelargoniums (in a peat base) with pink heather and some meadow saffron* (Colchicum autumnale).

*An antique tea caddy* (above right) *makes an excellent container for a flower display. To avoid leakage, this one was first fitted with a plastic box. The flowers are: heather, two roses, a nerine and a pelargonium leaf.*

*A classically-posed composition using only five African marigolds or gillyflowers* (Tagetes erecta), *with leaves and a few carefully chosen gourds.*

used in all-blue arrangements, depending on the season.

For variations in yellow, draw on African marigolds (gillyflowers, *Tagetes erecta*), yellow or orange dahlias, helenium, and, in spring, yellow daffodils, mimosa and buttercups. Another yellow composition could well be a few yellow roses or pom-pom dahlias, which are very suitable, and there are always medium-sized gladioli, or the yellow Cleopatra's needle or foxtail lily (*Eremurus bungei*). For really bright reds, there are roses, poppies and dozens of other red flowers.

*Dried flowers*

You can also achieve some interesting effects by using different kinds of dried flowers. Some intriguing possibilities in white and silver come to mind, using bleached and dried leaves which can be combined with traces of green or brown. 'Skeletonized' leaves look spectacular in dried flower arrangements; the seed pods of love-in-a-mist (*Nigella damascena*) make for a very subtle color combination. Nowadays, so many more varieties of flowers are being dried successfully that it is possible to produce stunning arrangements in blues, lilacs, yellows

A group of antique silver and silver-mounted scent bottles and snuff boxes (left) with a cut glass goblet holding an arrangement of a few roses, African marigolds or gillyflowers (Tagetes erecta), some ivy (Hedera), and fruity sprigs such as rose hips, hawthorn and elder.

Below: An autumnal display of fruits, sunflowers (Helianthus annuus) and one African marigold or gillyflower (Tagetes erecta).

and pinks, whatever your color preference. Don't forget the purple-tinted globe amaranth (*Gomphrena globosa*), the bluish purple *Catananche coerulea* or the various kinds of statice. The attractive green and mauve pendants of *Moluccella laevis* and *Nicandra physaloides* are also useful.

Dried flowers don't always have to be put in vases. They look just as effective bound together in an arrangement and then fixed to an unusual piece of driftwood, placed in a rustic basket, or attached to a plaque, where they will brighten the winter with their lasting colors.

# Pressed Flowers

Flower pressing is an absorbing hobby in any season, and it is one that will widen your horizons and knowledge of plant-life by increasing your awareness of the botanical world.

Pressed flowers can be used to make or enhance all kinds of decorative objects, but however you decide to use them, the same principles of preparation and design will apply.

*Equipment and materials*
*Blotting paper.* This is for the pressing. For economy, buy it in quantity rather than in single sheets. It can be dried and reused many times.
*Plenty of dry, clean newspaper.*
*A small bookbinding or flower press.* Useful when extra-heavy pressure is needed, but you can also use large, heavy books, or wooden boards, cut to about $350 \times 300$ mm ($14 \times 12$ in.), weighed down with bricks.

For mounting you need:
*Artist's card (white cardboard)* or fabric and cardboard.
*Adhesive.* Quick-drying, non-staining.
*Small watercolor paint brushes.*
*Sharp, pointed scissors.*
*Tweezers.* For lifting petals, etc.
*Razor blade.* For cutting material.
*Toothpicks or cocktail sticks.*
*Nail file.* The handle is used for lifting dried flowers; bend the tip upwards for moving flowers while arranging them.
*Picture frames.* These must be glazed and airtight.

*Selecting your flowers*
Pick only good flower specimens, and remember to pick plenty of small leaves and flowers as fillers. All flowers must be absolutely dry before pressing. It is best to gather them during dry spells in the middle of the day, after the dew has dried, as damp flowers will encourage mold.

Not all flowers are suitable for pressing. Avoid flowers of complex petal or head structure unless they can be dismantled, the petals pressed separately and then reassembled. Avoid fleshy, succulent plants too.

*Freesias are used in this arrangement. Leaves and stems from other plants give an overall effect of harmony and balance.*

Many flowers and leaves fade and discolor in time, but most will last about a year, if correctly pressed, mounted and kept in reasonable climatic conditions. Flowers which change color during pressing and particularly those which turn cream, beige, brown or black, will suffer only slight fading afterwards. Many orange, yellow or dark red flowers will last for several years without fading very much. Blue flowers tend to fade quickly, so avoid using them in long-term pictures.

Green leaves often fade quickly too, though some new and pale leaves turn black when pressed and can then be used safely. Gray and silver leaves show little color variation with time, and autumn leaves offer colorful and lasting effects. Bracken, ferns, lichens and ripe grasses all have permanent, stable coloring.

When planning a picture that you want to last, it's best to blend soft, pastel colors and rely on shape and pattern rather than on bold color. But when planning less long-lasting pictures, you can use all the bright colors you wish, enjoy summer bouquets in the winter and replace them when they fade.

## Pressing

First, flowers must be free from all external moisture. Then you must find the best way of pressing the flowers quite flat. Use small, sharp

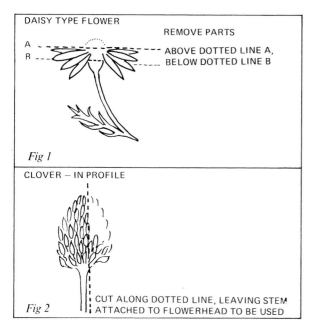

Fig 1

Fig 2

scissors to cut away the thickest parts, cutting carefully until the flower falls apart. You have to learn how much of a flower to remove to make it as flat as possible. With a daisy-type flower, this demolition will include at least the stem and the calyx and perhaps part of the center as well if it is hard. (See fig. 1.)

With a flower which can be pressed in profile, such as a clover, leave the stem but reduce the bulk of the head by cutting away at the back. (See fig. 2.)

Flowers such as honeysuckle and lupin (lupine) are unsuitable for cutting away and have to be taken apart, pressed and re-assembled.

*These pressed flowers have been put together with great care. Though the effect is one of rambling stems, leaves and flowers, it is pleasing to the eye. The frame gives just the right amount of white space around the group.*

67

*Table mats should be treated with a heatproof polyurethane varnish seal to make them durable and preserve their charm. Cut the mats from plywood or hardboard, and paint them. Then glue the plants on very carefully.*

Opposite: *this arrangement is mounted on fabric to give the background an interesting color and texture. Mount the fabric on a piece of stout card (pasteboard) before making the pressed flower picture.*

Roses, poppies and tulips can have their petals removed, pressed and then reassembled in their original form or as more simple flowers. The centers have to be pressed separately.

Fold blotting paper in half and arrange the flowers neatly in rows on one half of the inside sheet. Don't let the blooms overlap or touch each other, and flatten each flower as you work by pressing it down on the blotting paper. Label and date each sheet of blotting paper for easy reference and place it between wads of newspaper topped with heavy books or boards and, finally, weights. (See fig. 3.) Even distribution of weight is essential; all blooms on one sheet should be of the same thickness, and newspaper pads must be thick enough to give an even surface for each blotting folder.

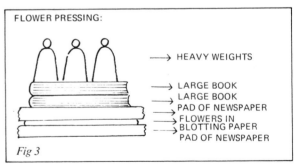

FLOWER PRESSING:

→ HEAVY WEIGHTS

→ LARGE BOOK
→ LARGE BOOK
→ PAD OF NEWSPAPER
→ FLOWERS IN
→ BLOTTING PAPER
  PAD OF NEWSPAPER

*Fig 3*

After about ten days, replace the newspaper pads with a fresh supply. Don't open the blotting pads but leave them undisturbed for at least a month. During this time, keep them in a warm, dry, well ventilated atmosphere, where they can be left until used.

68

Treat leaves in the same way as flowers. Press some stalks separately, choosing varying thicknesses, interesting lines and curves.

## Mounting

Work in a draught-free room with a moderate temperature and keep the flowers out of sunlight. From pressing and until the final sealing, the flowers are very delicate and will curl and damage if incorrectly handled. Remove them from the blotting paper sheets with tweezers.

Use flowers of uniform thickness. Mixing stout twigs and buds with fine flower petals can create difficulties, as when framed flowers must be pressed flat against the glass, and larger objects will create a space into which the flowers will wrinkle and shrink in time. Loosely arrange the flowers on their background first. Don't try to be too realistic: use your material to create other flowers (fig. 4), or adapt it to intensify color (fig. 5), or to add petals (fig. 6).

To glue flowers, apply adhesive in minute quantities with a toothpick or cocktail stick. Dot it in as many places as possible, so that the flowers are firmly and evenly fixed. The glue must not penetrate the flower from the underside.

## Making a picture

Use card (pasteboard) of any thickness; cut it to the size of your frame. Keep early attempts simple, without too much overlapping. The composition should provide a center of interest at some point, then lead the eye off to other details. Stems, leaves and curved sprays add to this latter effect, as shown in the sketches on page 73. Don't carry the work right to the edge of the card (pasteboard) but leave enough room for the frame.

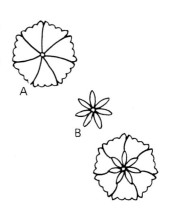

AN IMAGINARY FLOWER CREATED BY SUPERIMPOSING SMALL FLOWER B UPON LARGER FLOWER A

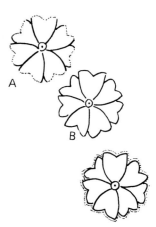

IDENTICAL BLOOM A PLACED OVER IDENTICAL BLOOM B TO INTENSIFY COLOUR

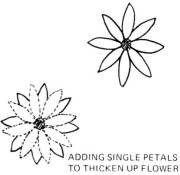

ADDING SINGLE PETALS TO THICKEN UP FLOWER

*You make these drink coasters in the same way as the table mats. Glue the flowers thoroughly and seal with adhesive film. Don't use flowers with thick centers or stems; they make the surface of the coasters bumpy.*

*Framing*

Good framing is vital if the picture is to last and keep its freshness. Secondhand frames save expense and lend themselves to painting with suitable colors, but make sure each one has a well fitting glass and that the frame is not bent or warped. When framed, the design must be pressed closely against the glass, so don't put a mount over your picture, as that will create a space between the flowers and the glass.

The picture must be completely airtight and damp-proof. The best way to achieve this is to use the original backing of the design as the intermediate layer and add a piece of hardboard cut exactly to size as a final frame backing. Secure the hardboard backing firmly to the frame with panel pins and cover the joined edges with adhesive paper strips. When reusing an old frame, brush out the inside rims to remove dust and fragments. Check again for cleanliness after inserting a new picture, before backing and sealing. When completed, the picture should be hung out of direct sunlight or any strong light.

Make paperweights with glass mounts, backed by flowers, on card (pasteboard) or cloth. Take your time when making these attractive ornaments, as bullseye glass mounts will magnify dirty marks and untidy edges as well as the flowers.

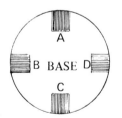

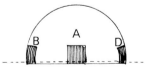

The decorated base for a glass paperweight is inserted face downwards and secured with four evenly-spaced pieces of adhesive tape. When the backing material is firmly glued in position, cut through the adhesive tape as indicated by the dotted line.

## Drink coasters

You can either make your own mats from wood, hardboard or cork, or buy cheap, plain coasters and decorate them. You can even use suitable can lids. Cut a paper or fabric base, glue it to the coaster and arrange your flowers on it. When making the design, avoid thick stems, which will make a bumpy surface. Cover the coasters with heavy household transparent adhesive film as used for covering shelves. After covering, seal the edges completely with strong glue so that the coasters can be wiped clean after use.

## Paperweights

Glass mounts are sold in crafts shops; generally there are two types, the bullseye and the flat type. Turn the glass mount upside down, make sure that the underside of the surface is clean, then insert the decorated base and secure it in four places with narrow strips of adhesive tape, as shown in the drawing. Back the base with felt or leather, sticking it to the glass rim with strong glue to seal it. When dry, peel the tape away from the glass.

## Bookmarks

For the single strip type of bookmark (below left) you need a strip of ribbon 30 × 300 mm (1¼ × 12 in.). Glue the design on it firmly, taking care that the adhesive does not stain the ribbon. Keep the arrangement well within the border of the ribbon, and protect it with a coat of heavy transparent film, in the same way as for coasters. Allow a generous margin all round when cutting, and trim away the surplus with scissors. For the double bookmark, a narrow ribbon is superimposed on a contrasting wider one.

## Table mats

Mats can be cut from plywood or hardboard. Stick the material very firmly to the mats. Use leaves and grasses rather than flowers and petals for this kind of work, so that the finished design is flat.

When you have completed your design, spray or paint the mats with at least three coats of polyurethane gloss varnish, which will dry with a hard and heatproof finish. When the first coat of varnish becomes tacky, check that the design is firmly stuck down.

*You make these bookmarks from ribbon and small pressed flowers. Use glue sparingly to prevent it from seeping through the ribbon and leaving ugly stains on the underside.*

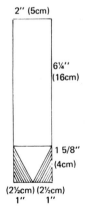

2″ (5cm)

6¼″ (16cm)

1 5/8″ (4cm)

(2½cm) (2½cm)
1″    1″

*Bookmarks can also be made from card (pasteboard). Cut a piece to the shape of this drawing. Mount the flowers carefully on it, and seal with adhesive film for protection.*

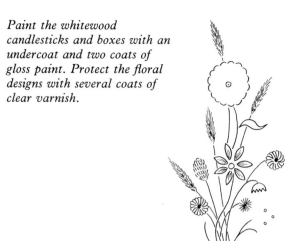

*Paint the whitewood candlesticks and boxes with an undercoat and two coats of gloss paint. Protect the floral designs with several coats of clear varnish.*

*Flowers on wood*

The small boxes and candlesticks on the left are whitewood items, bought from a crafts shop, that have been painted with an undercoat and two coats of gloss paint, and then decorated with pressed flowers. The floral design is protected with several coats of clear varnish. Some flowers and leaves can be affected by the varnish, which can cause swift loss of color. Do a little testing first by gluing flowers on a spare piece of wood and covering them carefully with clear varnish. Leave them uncovered for about three weeks to test for color fastness. Alternatively, you can play safe and use flowers and leaves which will show little color change, such as cream and beige petals and white or autumn leaves.

Stick all the items very securely and press down any loose bits with a cocktail stick while the varnish is still tacky.

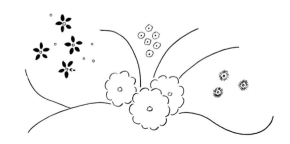

## Greetings cards

Use thin card (pasteboard) cut to fit a standard size envelope, but don't use black card (pasteboard) for this work as it looks misty when the adhesive sheeting is applied. Cover the card (pasteboard) with light transparent film, allowing a generous overlap on the edges, then trim.

*A small cardboard strut is mounted on the back of the animal cards by gluing the shaded part to the card.*

74

*Writing case and address book*

Here, pressed flowers have been used on soft plastic. The design on the left is done in white flowers and leaves, which means that there will be no fading. As always, the design was arranged before being stuck down.

These two items were covered with the non-adhesive transparent film used for covering maps and books; this gives a glass-like finish ideal for plastic. Take the film over the edges to the inside of the covers, and seal firmly with adhesive tape.

*The two examples of pressed flower pictures (below) have been arranged with plenty of contrast in shape and color. Flowers have only been laid over other flowers and leaves where they are very flat.*

*Pressed flowers are mounted on to the soft plastic of this address book and writing case.*

# Stone on Stone

Painting stones does not sound like a very exciting or creative pastime! But if you look through these pages, you will see that it is far from dull. This chapter also takes the pebble-painting theme a little further by showing you how to glue stones together to make decorative figures and animals, some of them not painted at all, and others with only a little paint or varnish added.

Collect as many different stones as you can, big and small, wherever you go. It's wise, when stone hunting, to look for two, four or six similar pebbles, so that you can match them

*These two animals are very different in construction. The larger one's tiny pebbles should be as flat as possible. Try to get a subtle blend of color and tone. First stick the tiny stones on the forehead, then work backwards from there. Make the small tortoise from six stones.*

*This fine fellow is full of self-confidence. Some stones will stand up on their own without any assistance. Others can be propped up with tiny stone feet.*

76

*A stone-faced troglodyte.*

*Here is a whole family of tortoises. They are all decorated with fine lines, which need practice. The only colors used are white, black and gold, yet they are very striking. The painter has studied the natural colors and stripes of the stones, and has featured them in the overall design.*

later. You need stones for bodies, heads, eyes, ears, noses, arms, feet and tails, as you can see from the illustrations in this chapter.

If you travel a lot, you will have access to a wider variety of stones, even if you do have to pay excess airfare baggage costs! The stones used here are from Europe, the United States and Canada. You might also be able to get hold of the smooth coal black stones which are to be found on some of the Greek islands, the snow white stones of Italy and the Mediterranean coast, rosy red stones from the Baltic coast and finely bored pebbles from northern France, to name a few. Ask your friends to bring some stones back with them from their holidays and you will soon have a varied collection of exotic material.

*Tools and materials*
*Adhesive.* For long-lasting stone figures, you will need a two-part epoxy resin. This is usually available in packs of two tubes, the resin and the hardener, perhaps with a spatula for mixing them. Follow the manufacturer's instructions carefully, and remember that all powerful glues must be used with care. Eyes,

hair and skin are especially vulnerable, and small children should never use these adhesives without adult supervision. Several other weaker adhesives are suitable for semi-permanent work and for children to use. The clear cellulose-acetate type adhesives, used for most craftwork, dry clear quickly and set very hard. Since each shop tends to stock a different type, try those available locally. Trial and error is the only way to discover which glue is right for a certain texture or size of stone, and for the way each one will be stuck.

If you are the sort of person who likes to change your mind while making a creature, don't use a fast-drying glue or you will not be able to change short legs for long ones, or move the position of the eyes. At first you will probably use too much glue: you can scrape off the excess with a knife or a razor blade and you will soon learn how much to apply.

*Non-hardening modeling clay.* This is invaluable for fixing and holding stones together while they are being stuck. The ducks below had some non-hardening modeling clay round the neck and under the bill to support them while the glue was drying. If you are gluing a

*A bird made from flat pebbles with tiny, round feet.*

*These ducks' bodies are plump, round stones. If you choose a stone with your animal's shape, its character will be more realistic. Heads, beaks and tails for animals like these are best held in place with non-hardening modeling clay, before gluing. When painting fine detail, as on the yellow duck, put a book under your painting hand to support it and keep it very still during decoration.*

*These fishes would be rather dull without their scales. You need to practice this kind of detailed painting on similar stones. Use a fine sable brush. Keep your hand still and work slowly. Great care has been taken in painting these fins, scales and features to make them really fishlike.*

Below: *Support the trees carefully with non-hardening modeling clay before gluing. It is sometimes easier to paint the leaves before assembling the stones. The fruit are tiny pieces of gravel, painted red and glued on before varnishing the whole woodland scene.*

figure containing five or more stones, glue them together in stages. If the non-hardening modeling clay leaves a greasy stain on the stone, these marks can be removed with a suitable solvent – ask at the chemist's (pharmacy) or crafts shop what to use.

*Paints.* You don't have to paint your stones, and sometimes they look better unpainted. If you do want to add color, brush the paint on as sparingly as possible, using just enough to give a good, opaque color and no more. Use poster or acrylic colors, and use light colors as much as you can. Don't use too much black because most of the stones will be a dark color already. It's usually best to paint stones after gluing them, though in some cases (when adding a set of teeth to a crocodile, for example) you will have to paint them first. Support your painting

*This little fellow has been given a black coat and nose to enhance his character.*

hand with a book when painting fine lines.

*Varnish.* The use of varnish is a matter for personal taste. You may think that plain, unadorned stones are best since they show their natural beauty, but a coat of clear varnish on an unpainted pebble does bring out the natural texture more strongly than a mere wash and polish. The color of a varnished stone will look as fresh as if it was under water.

*Paint brushes.* Buy the finest (sizes 00 and 0) and softest available. Work out your pattern roughly first, and get used to painting thin lines. Restrict yourself to a few carefully chosen lines, strokes and dots. If you use non-water enamels and acrylics, don't forget to thin them down with the recommended thinner.

*Board.* A large pastry board makes a good working suface which can be set aside when you want to use the main table for something else.

*Ideas for working*

There are many more possible figures to be made than little stone men and miniature garden gnomes, and stylized animal pebble figures can look very striking, as you can see above.

The kinds of stones needed to make ducks, imaginary birds, tortoises and mice are the easiest to find, as these animals are mostly composed of oval or flat pebbles, which are common to most beaches. You will also have

collected some unusually shaped pebbles, and if one of these will not stand up by itself, then add some small pebble feet, or choose the flattest side as the base and stand it firmly on that.

When working, don't think that you must only make the animal you thought of in the first place. First ideas are often not very good, either because they don't fit the actual stones or because some new and more appropriate idea takes over. Half an ape, a misshapen parrot or a poodle can quite easily turn into a lively cat, a duck or a spaniel. Often, you will produce crazy mixtures that are great fun, like a zebra-goose, an elephant-pig or a snake-alligator. Don't decide rigidly at the beginning what your stones are going to be, because it may be impossible to find exactly the stone you need to make the creature you had imagined. Instead, draw your inspiration from the material before you. Look for matching shapes among the chaotic mass of stones. Let a figure stand, for days if necessary, without trying to finish it. Wait until your inspiration has done its work, and then you will know that the finished animal is absolutely right.

*These snappers look much more dangerous than they are. To make sure the jaws stay open while gluing, stick a piece of non-hardening modeling clay inside the mouth. Paint the body and teeth before gluing and everything else afterwards.*

# Dried Flowers and Seeds

Flowers are always beautiful, but they are not always cheap, especially in winter. This is one of the reasons why dried flowers are so popular. They are lovely in themselves and their colors last right through the darkest months, making delightful arrangements and decorations for the table, for Christmas and to hang around the house. Dried seeds of sycamore, ash, alder, different types of fir and larch cone, acorn cups and beech seeds are all to be found in most parks and fields in autumn. Gather all these, and teazels, pine needles, oat grains and plenty of grasses, all of which will add variety to any

Pine-cones

*Make each owl (left) by interlocking the spikes of two pine cones, gluing them together and varnishing them carefully. The nose and ears are felt cut to size. The eyes are yellow felt with shiny black cardboard disks at the center. The lichen-covered log makes an excellent perch.*

Ash

design.

*Drying flowers*
Seeds and cones, of course, dry naturally, and they require no further attention once they are really dry, but you will also need a few dried flowers for your work, and these have to be dried carefully. You can buy these cheaply from florists and crafts shops, but it's much more fun to gather and dry your own.

Many (but not all) garden plants dry well, and there are plenty of wild flowers to look for on rambles in the country, yarrow, cow parsley,

tansy, ribwort, and many more. Experiment with drying what you find and you will soon discover which ones are best for your purpose.

There are three basic ways of preserving flowers, leaves and grasses. They can be air dried, placed in a special drying powder of some kind, or preserved in glycerine. No matter which method you use, always cut the flowers to be treated on a warm day and always pick flowers *before* they come into full bloom.

*Air drying*
Air drying is perhaps the easiest method of all if

*This tortoise's body is a large pine cone cut in half, with the varnished base on top. Add feet for stability. A walnut makes a lifelike head. The eyes are felt and cardboard.*

83

Dill

Larch

*Make the large star by fixing yarrow stalks between two cardboard disks with glue. When dry, add an inner star made from horse oak leaves. Four seeds from a dark pine cone, four oat ears and an acorn in its cup complete the decoration.*

you have enough space for it. Pick the flowers and remove the leaves, as they will wither when dried and will also become tangled.

Make small bunches of flowers. If you make large bunches, they will get mixed up with each other when they are dry. Tie them by the stems with string and hang them (each bunch well apart) heads down on a line in a cool, airy, dry and dark place.

As the flowers dry they will shrink, so from time to time check that the string is still tight so that the flowers are held securely.

Large-headed flowers can be air dried in a vase. Choose flowers that have a strong stem: you can always substitute a wire stem if the flower's own stem doesn't look strong enough to support the head.

Hydrangeas dry well, but they need slightly different treatment. Stand them in about 50 mm (2 in.) of water in a warm room and hang them to dry when all the water has been absorbed.

Grasses may take only about a week to air dry, but larger flowers can take much longer. You will learn in time exactly when they are quite dry and can be stored in a dry place or

84

Alder

*Three pieces of wood, glued together, form the body of this decoration. Cover the star shape with seed pods that have been glued in place. A small cluster of everlasting flowers makes a centerpiece; attach a flower at each point.*

Sycamore

used for decoration.

Not all flowers are suitable for air drying, but, for example, mimosa, achillea, *Helichrysum bracteatum* (strawflower) and gypsophila are all flowers which can be air dried successfully. There are many other flowers which can be dried too. It does no harm to experiment with what you have in your garden.

### Drying with powders

Borax and silica gel are two of the best known drying powders and you can buy these at most pharmacies. Flowers dried by this method retain much of their original color but they have to be kept in a dry atmosphere once they have been dried. To powder dry flowers, a layer of powder should be put in a box or tin, and the flowers placed on top of this layer. More powder should then be poured on top and between the petals so that the flower is completely covered and the moisture will be totally absorbed by the powder.

Most flowers take about two or three days to dry by this method, but the time will vary depending on the moisture in the flower and the thickness of the petals, so you must test each

*Decorate the spikes around the head of this teazel with large, red-painted seeds. Attach dried leaves from sweetcorn (maize) to the stem to give a better shape to the overall design.*

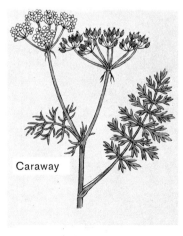

Caraway

flower from time to time by removing a little of the powder and looking at the petals. The powder can always be replaced if the petals are not quite dry. Don't leave them in the powder for too long without inspecting them or the petals will become so brittle that they will completely disintegrate when you take them out! Stems become very brittle, so much so that it is best to dry only the heads and replace the stems with florist's wire.

*Preserving in glycerine*
This is the traditional method for preserving autumn leaves, but you can also use it for flowers. Gather autumn leaves *before* they begin to change color, not after, or they will not be able to absorb the liquid.

Place the stems in water for a few hours before placing in the glycerine, and split thick, woody stems so that the liquid can travel up them more easily. Mix one part of glycerine to two parts of water, stand the stems in this liquid, and leave them for about two or three weeks. During this time, the leaves will change color and you will have some lasting foliage for your arrangements.

Two of these examples show how to add tiny artificial flowers to a teazel head to great effect. Delicate decoration of this kind is very successful. The separate flower stalks added to the top right-hand teazel head are also effective. Color each stalk with white or copper paint. The lower decoration on the left is a teazel head with silver seed clusters and bronze ash seeds. Red-painted ash seeds have been added to the teazel on the lower right.

## Tools and materials

The simplicity of this craft means that very few tools or materials are needed:

*Pruning shears.* These are best for cutting flower clusters from stems.

*Adhesive.* Use a clear, quick-drying adhesive.

*Scissors.* For trimming grasses, stems and ribbons, and for cutting twine.

*An awl.* For boring holes in seeds. (A knitting needle will do.)

*Twine or thread.* For hanging up the decorations. Florist's wire can also be used and, for more festive arrangements, brightly colored ribbons will look attractive.

*Paints.* Very little paint should be used, as the natural colors usually look best, but a touch of color is sometimes needed. In the process of drying, flowers lose some of their color, but they still retain their beautiful shapes and the more subtle gray and brown colors are very lovely in their own quiet way. Large plants like teazels and bullrushes need no extra color, though sometimes people do spray them gold or silver. Smaller plants may benefit from the addition of a little colored paint. You can use poster or acrylic colors, and white, bronze,

Thistle

The top decoration shows the original effect gained by fixing a number of acorn cups containing tiny, artificial flowers in an open larch cone. Add hogweed stems, painted white. The lower decoration consists of white-painted teazels, glued into a star shape, with yarrow stalks fixed between them. A beech-nut pod forms the hub. Artificial flowers are arranged in a circle around it. Make the star blossoms on the left and right from a combination of pine-cone scales and fir or pine needles. Cut the scales from the cone with secateurs (pruning shears). Glue the needles between two cardboard disks, then glue the scales to both sides. Complete with oat ears and dried flowers.

silver or gold spray paints.
*Felt.* Useful for adding eyes and ears to animals.

### Making fir cone figures

These are perhaps the easiest of all figures to make, and children will enjoy making strange animals with fir cones.

Simply stick a few fir cones to each other, by gluing and interlocking the spines. Add felt eyes, noses and ears to make strange birds, monsters, owls (as on page 82) or a tortoise (as on page 83). Stand these little animals on a piece of branch or in a woodland setting of pine needles or among a few dried flowers. You can make a fir cone open up by drying it slowly in the oven.

### Stars with a cone center

A pine or larch cone will provide the hub of a star, and the grasses or flower stems can then be stuck to the scales of the cone. The star may be sprayed bronze or otherwise colored so that it stands out against the background, or it can be left in its natural colors.

Yarrow

*Make the wreath at the top around a wire circle. The materials are grasses, pine cones, beech nuts, painted teazels cut in half, and everlasting flowers. The lower wreath is a circle of pine cone scales, larch needles and tiny dry flowers. Use a large cardboard disk as a base. The left-hand design is a circle of beech-nut scales with a center of greenery, tiny dry flowers, and a large walnut. The right-hand wreath is built on a wire circle. Materials are beech nuts, ribwort, and tiny dry flowers.*

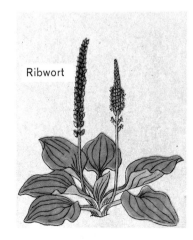
Ribwort

## Star blossoms

As you can see from the illustration on page 88, these hanging decorations are simple yet effective. You could make several to hang in a group on a wall. They can be made from a combination of pine cone scales and fir or pine needles. First, cut the scales from the cone with pruning shears. Attach a piece of twine, for hanging, to a 12 mm (½ in.) disk of cardboard and glue on pine needles radiating out from the center of the card. Take a second cardboard disk of the same size, cover it with adhesive and attach it to the first disk, so that both the twine

and the pine needles are firmly held between the two disks. When the adhesive has dried, glue cone scales to both sides of the double disk. For effect, add a few maize grains, and a small larch cone in the center. Many other variations are possible. Make colorful centers of bronzed thistles, artificial flowers, oat grains, alder cones, acorn cups, or dried flower heads.

## Thistles and teazels
Thistles and teazels can be sprayed with paint or left in their natural state.

*Pot-pourri, twirl and lavender corn dollies. The pot-pourri (left) is the same basic shape as the twirl, but without the heads on the corn. Put a small sachet of pot-pourri inside the dolly before finishing it off with a four-straw plait and pink ribbon. Make the twirl (center) from a three-straw plait and a five-straw plait. Once you can make the twirl, you will be able to produce most other corn dollies without difficulty. Use six straws to get a rounder lavender dolly (right). Insert a small lavender sachet before finishing off.*

# Corn Dollies

Corn dolly making is a very ancient rural craft which has seen a popular revival in the past few years. With the help of these designs and instructions, corn dollies can be made quite easily.

A corn dolly is a traditional symbol of fertility. In the past, men working in the harvest fields used to plait and weave corn dollies as a means of giving thanks to the goddesses of the earth and fertility. When the harvest was over, the dollies would be taken home and kept warm and dry in order to safeguard the harvest for the following year.

Special hollow-straw corn is used to make corn dollies. Those in this chapter have been made with either Maris Widgeon, Elite Lepeuple or Flymel. Straw kits can be bought from crafts shops, but if a local farmer grows the right kind of wheat, he may let you have sufficient for your needs.

Straw should be cut when it is nearly ripe: the only part needed for making corn dollies is the length from the corn ear to the first joint in the straw. Cut the straw just above the first joint, and remove the grass sheath covering the stalk. Make sure that the straw is quite dry before storing it in a warm, dry place: an airing cupboard is ideal.

*Tools and materials*

You will need: a pair of sharp scissors; corn-colored button thread; various ribbons for decoration. Ribbons play a traditional part in the history of corn dollies: red ribbon symbolizes a poppy in the cornfield; green, the young corn; yellow, the heat of the sun; blue, a clear sky; purple, clover; and white symbolizes purity.

*General instructions*

Before starting work on any of these models, all straw must be made pliable by soaking it in water. The complete length, including the head, should be soaked in hot water for 20 minutes. Cover the corn with a damp cloth to keep it moist while you are working. Any damp corn left over should be thoroughly dried before storage.

When a straw is nearly used up, or if it should break, you will need to join it to a new one. To do this, cut the used straw back to the last corner of the work, insert the thin end of the new straw into its hollow, and continue working.

When a corn dolly is complete, hang it up to dry in a warm place, head downwards.

Three-straw and five-straw plaits are the basis on which many corn dollies are made, so details for their construction are given first. Whenever a model requires one of these plaits you will need to refer back to these instructions.

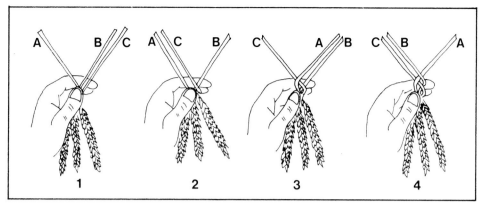

Above: *Stages in making the Welsh border fan.*

Below: *Stages in making a five-straw plait.*

*Three-straw plait*

1. Soak the straws in hot water for 15–20 minutes.
2. Select three straws and tie them together tightly with thread just above the heads.
3. Holding the straws in the left hand, commence the plait by keeping straws B and C together and bending them away from straw A (fig. 1).

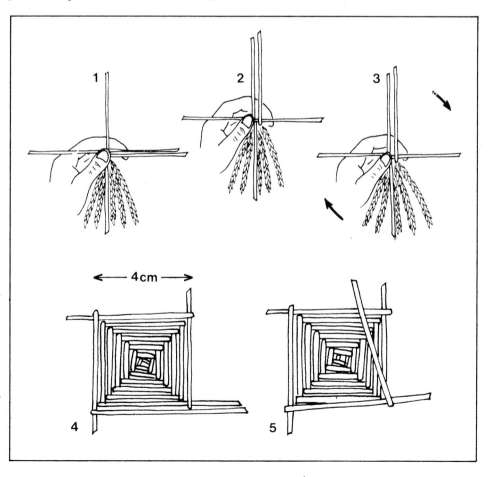

4. Bend straw *C* towards you and lay it across straw *B* so that it is now beside straw *A* (fig. 2).
5. Bend straw *A* towards you and lay it across straw *C* so that it is now beside straw *B* (fig. 3).
6. Bend straw *B* towards you and lay it across straw *A* so that it is now beside straw *C* (fig. 4).
7. Repeat steps 4 to 6 until the plait is 120 mm (4¾ in.) long. Tie off the ends with thread and trim the straws 20 mm (¾ in.) above the tie.

*Five-straw plait*
1. Soak the straws in hot water for 15–20 minutes.
2. Select five straws and tie them together tightly with thread just above the heads.
3. Hold the straws in the left hand and place the straws in the position shown in fig. 1.
4. Take the upper straw from the 3 o'clock position, bend it under and over the lower straw and lay it alongside the 12 o'clock straw (fig. 2).
5. Turn the work clockwise so that the two straws are at the 3 o'clock position again (fig. 3).
6. Repeat steps 4 and 5 so that the work gradually increases in a square form. Continue until the square being formed is 40 mm (1½ in.) across (fig. 4).
7. Take the upper straw from the 3 o'clock position, bend it under and over the lower straw and lay it to the left of the 12 o'clock straw (fig. 5).
8. Turn the work clockwise so that the two straws are at the 3 o'clock position again.
9. Take the lower straw from the 3 o'clock position, bend it over the upper straw and lay it to the left of the 12 o'clock straw.
10. Turn the work clockwise so that the two straws are at the 3 o'clock position again.
11. Repeat steps 9 and 10 so that the work gradually decreases until the straws meet in the middle. Bend the straws up and tie them tightly with thread. Trim the straws to 20 mm (¾ in.) above the tie.

**Twirl corn dolly**
Make a three-straw plait and form it into a loop. Make a five-straw plait, tie on the looped three-straw plait and decorate with red ribbon.

**Pot-pourri dolly**
Make a five-straw plait around a small sachet of pot-pourri. Complete the dolly with a four-straw plait and pink ribbon.

*Four-straw plait*
1. Select four straws and tie them together tightly with thread just above the heads, then cut off the heads.
2. Keeping two straws together, spread out the remaining two straws at equal intervals (fig. 1).
3. Take the lower straw from the 3 o'clock position, bend it up over the upper straw and lay it on top and to the left of the 11 o'clock straw (fig. 2).
4. Turn the work clockwise so that the two straws are at the 3 o'clock position (fig. 3).
5. Repeat steps 3 and 4 until the work is 100 mm (4 in.) long. Tie off with thread and trim the ends of the straw just above the tie.

**Lavender dolly** *(six-straw plait)*
1. Select six straws without heads. Tie them tightly together 10 mm (⅜ in.) above the thin ends. Keeping two straws together, spread out the remaining straws at equal intervals (fig. 1).
2. Take the lower straw from the 2 o'clock position, bend it up and over the upper straw and lay it on top and to the left of the 12 o'clock straw (fig. 2).
3. Turn the work clockwise until the two straws are at the 2 o'clock position (fig. 3).
4. Repeat steps 2 and 3 four times to complete the round.
5. Take the lower straw from the 2 o'clock position, bend it up and over the upper straw and lay it alongside the 12 o'clock straw (fig. 4).
6. Turn the work clockwise until the two straws are at the 2 o'clock position.
7. Repeat steps 5 and 6 so that the sides of the work gradually increase. Continue until the side of the work is 30 mm (1¼ in.) long (fig. 5).
8. Take the lower straw from the 2 o'clock position, bend it up and over the upper straw and lay it on top and to the left of the 12 o'clock straw (fig. 6).
9. Turn the work clockwise until the two straws are at the 2 o'clock position.

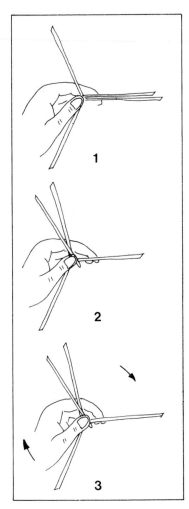

Above: *Stages in making a three-straw plait.*

Right: *This delightful corn maiden has a skirt of corn heads, arms made from a four-straw plait, a bonnet made from a six-straw plait, and a skirt hoop made from a three-straw plait. Complete the dolly with pink ribbon bows.*

10. Repeat steps 8 and 9 so that the sides of the work gradually decrease until the straws meet at the center. Before this stage is reached, insert a lavender bag inside the dolly. When the straws meet, bend them up, tie off, and trim the ends 20 mm (¾ in.) above the tie.

11. Finish off by tying on a loop and bow of purple ribbon.

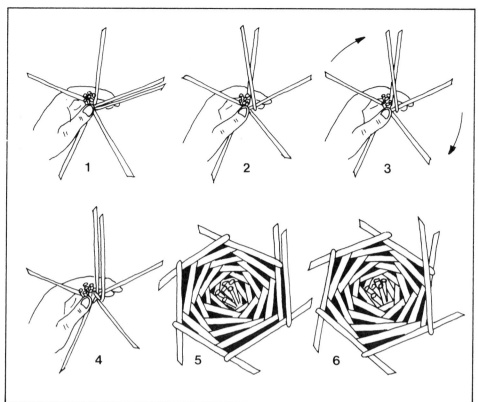

Above: *Stages in making a lavender dolly.*

## Corn maiden

*Hoop for skirt*
Make a three-straw plait 140 mm (5½ in.) long after removing the corn heads. Form it into a loop and decorate with ribbon at the tie.

*Arms*
Make a four-straw plait 100 mm (4 in.) long.

*Bonnet (six-straw plait)*
1. Select six straws. Tie them together tightly just above the heads. Keeping two straws together, spread out the remaining straws at equal intervals (fig. 1).
2. Take the lower straw from the 2 o'clock position, bend it up and over the upper straw and lay it on top and to the left of the 12 o'clock straw (fig. 2).
3. Turn the work clockwise so that the two straws are at the 2 o'clock position (fig. 3).
4. Repeat steps 2 and 3 four times to complete the round.

5.   Take the lower straw from the 2 o'clock position, bend it up and over the upper straw and lay it alongside the 12 o'clock straw (fig. 4).

6.   Turn the work clockwise so that the two straws are at the 2 o'clock position.

7.   Repeat steps 5 and 6 so that the sides of the work gradually increase. Continue in this manner for four complete rounds.

8.   Take the lower straw from the 2 o'clock position, bend it up and over the upper straw and lay it on top and to the left of the 12 o'clock straw (fig. 5).

9.   Turn the work clockwise so that the two straws are at the 2 o'clock position.

10.   Repeat steps 8 and 9 so that the sides of the work gradually decrease. Continue in this manner for four complete rounds.

11.   To form the brim of the bonnet, the sides of the work must again be increased, so repeat steps 5 and 6 for five complete rounds.

12.   Tie off the last two straws to keep the work together. Trim the remaining straws and decorate with pink ribbon.

*Body*

1.   Select 20 straws and, holding them loosely together in one hand, with the heads pointing downwards, support the heads with the palm of the other hand. Allow the heads to level off, and

Below: *Stages in making a six-straw plait for the corn maiden's bonnet.*

Right: *Stages in making the corn maiden's body.*

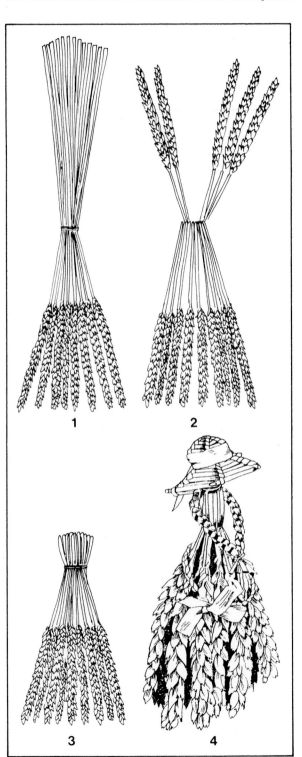

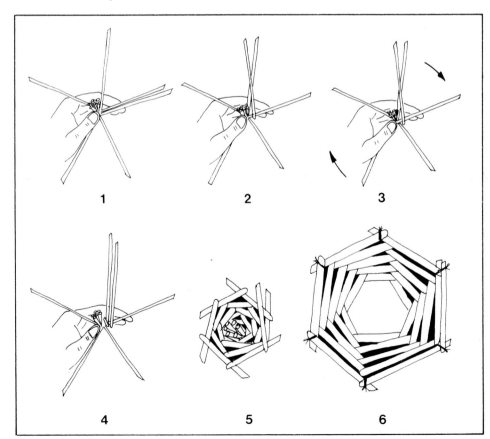

then tie the straws together tightly at a point 150 mm (6 in.) above the ends of the heads. Trim the ends of the straws 150 mm (6 in.) above the tie (fig. 1).

2. Turn the work upside down and bring the heads down evenly to form the skirt (fig. 2).

3. Tie the straws together tightly 20 mm ($\frac{3}{4}$ in.) from the top to form the head (fig. 3).

4. Lift up five straws and insert the arms. Replace the five straws and make a tie 40 mm ($1\frac{1}{2}$ in.) below the top to form the waist. To hold the arms in position, bring the ends of the four-straw plait together and tie at the front.

5. Fit the hoop over the skirt and put on the bonnet. If necessary, trim the ends of straws at the base of the skirt so that the corn maiden will stand upright.

**Welsh border fan**

1. Make a three-straw plait.

2. Take another three straws and tie them together tightly with thread just above the heads. Lay them on a flat surface with one straw to the left and two to the right (fig. 1).

3. Lift up the outer right straw, insert a new straw and replace the outer right straw (fig. 2).

*The Welsh border fan. Also known as the Herefordshire fan, this corn dolly must be made on a flat surface. Although it is slightly more difficult to make, you will probably agree that the final result is well worth the effort.*

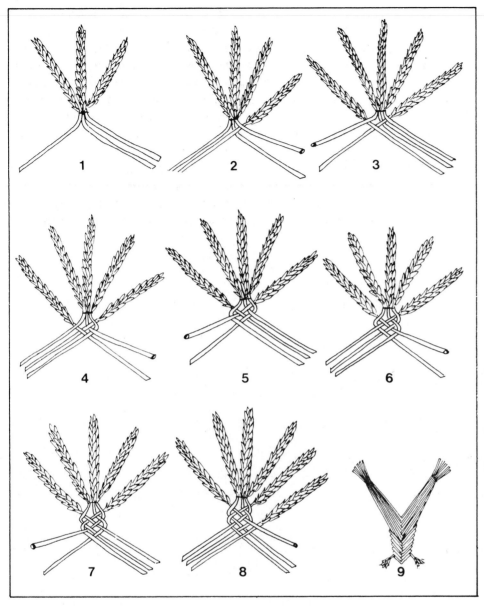

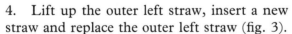

*Above: Stages in making a four-straw plait.*

from stage 4 (fig. 8).

9. Continue with stages 4 to 8 until ten straws have been added to each side of the original three straws, then continue with the 'locking stitches' until the side of the fan is 120 mm (4¾ in.) long. Draw up the two sides and tie them with thread 50 mm (2 in.) below the tops (fig. 9).

10. Tie on the three-straw plait and decorate the fan with ribbon.

## Swan

Based on five-straw weaving, the swan is made by increasing and decreasing the size of the plait.

1. Select five thin straws and tie them together tightly just above the heads. Cut off the heads, and, holding the work in the left hand, place the straws in the position indicated in fig. 1.

2. Take the upper straw from the 3 o'clock position, bend it under and over the lower straw and lay it alongside the 12 o'clock straw (fig. 2).

3. Turn the work clockwise so that the two straws are at the 3 o'clock position again (fig. 3).

4. Repeat steps 2 and 3 so that the work gradually increases in a square form. Continue until the square is 15 mm (⅝ in.) across (fig. 4).

5. Take the upper straw from the 3 o'clock position, bend it under and over the lower straw and lay it to the left of the 12 o'clock straw (fig. 5).

6. Turn the work clockwise so that the two straws are at the 3 o'clock position again.

7. Take the lower straw from the 3 o'clock position, bend it over the upper straw and lay it to the left of the 12 o'clock straw.

8. Turn the work clockwise so that the two straws are at the 3 o'clock position again.

9. Repeat steps 7 and 8 so that the work gradually decreases. When the side of the square has decreased to 10 mm (⅜ in.), continue plaiting, keeping the square the same size until the work is 120 mm (4¾ in.) long.

10. The work must now be increased, so repeat steps 2 and 3 until the square formed is 55 mm (2⅛ in.) across (fig. 6).

4. Lift up the outer left straw, insert a new straw and replace the outer left straw (fig. 3).

5. Lift up the second straw from the edge on the right-hand side, bend it round the outer straw, lay it alongside the left-hand straws and replace the lifted straw (fig. 4).

6. Lift up the second straw from the edge on the left-hand side, bend it round the outer straw, lay it alongside the right-hand straws and replace the lifted straw (fig. 5).

7. Repeat steps 5 and 6 (known as 'locking stitches') once more (figs. 6 and 7).

8. Lift up the outer right straw, insert a new straw, replace the lifted straw and proceed as

**1**

**2**

**3**

**4**　　**5**　　**6**

Above: *The swan* (left) *needs the same five-straw weaving as the twirl. You can get the right shape by increasing and decreasing the plait. A piece of wire runs through the swan to keep its shape sturdy. Make the glory braid* (right) *on a flat surface and finish with red ribbon. A traditional decoration for harvest suppers.*

Left: *Stages in making the swan.*

11. The work must now be decreased, so repeat steps 5 and 6 once and then repeat steps 7 and 8 until the straws meet in the middle. Just before the straws meet, insert a strong wire through the body and neck so that it protrudes 15 mm ($\frac{5}{8}$ in.) from the beginning of the work. Tie off the end of the work and trim the straws and wire.

12. Bend the neck into an S-shape. Push a short straw over the wire that protrudes at the beginning of the work. Bend the straw and tie it back to form the swan's beak.

## Glory braid

A traditional corn dolly that is much favoured as decoration at harvest suppers.

1. Select 12 straws and tie them together tightly just above the heads.
2. Place the work on a flat surface in the position shown in fig. 1.
3. Bend straw *C1* over *B* straws and lay it alongside straw *A4*.

Bend straw *C2* over *B* straws and lay it alongside straw *C1*.

Bend straw *C3* over *B* straws and lay it alongside straw *C2*.

Bend straw *C4* over *B* straws and lay it alongside straw *C3* (fig. 2).

4. Bend straw *A4* over *C* straws and lay it alongside straw *B1*.

Bend straw *A3* over *C* straws and lay it alongside straw *A4*.

Bend straw *A2* over *C* straws and lay it alongside straw *A3*.

Bend straw *A1* over *C* straws and lay it alongside straw *A2* (fig. 3).

5. Bend straw *B1* over *A* straws and lay it alongside straw *C4*.

Bend straw *B2* over *A* straws and lay it alongside straw *B1*.

Bend straw *B3* over *A* straws and lay it alongside straw *B2*.

Bend straw *B4* over *A* straws and lay it alongside straw *B3* (fig. 4).

6. Repeat steps 3 to 5 until the plait is 100 mm (4 in.) long (fig. 5).

7. Turn the work over and bend the center group of four straws down to the back of the

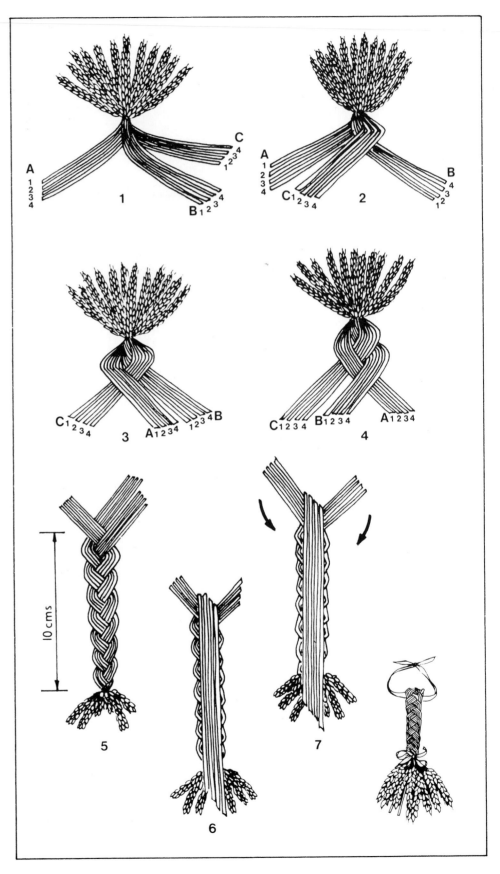

98

Left: *Stages in making the glory braid.*

*Wedmore wheel. Designed with the aim of incorporating traditional weaving in a modern design, the wheel is constructed from twelve glory braids linked on a circular wire and held in position with a three-straw plait.*

plait (fig. 6).

8. Repeat this procedure with the other two groups of four straws (fig. 7).

9. Tie all three groups of straws down on the plait at the first tie.

10. Trim the straws and decorate the dolly with red ribbon.

### Common faults

Few people are able to make a perfect corn dolly at the first attempt, so do not despair if your own first effort does not live up to your expectations. Here are the three most common faults and how to correct them.

1. *Corn dolly looks loose.* This means you are being too timid when plaiting straws. Use more pressure with your thumbs when placing the straw in the 12 o'clock position.

2. *Corn dolly looks squashed.* You are using too much pressure with your thumbs when placing the straw at the 12 o'clock position. Just be a little more gentle.

3. *Splitting corn.* Either your corn is not being soaked for long enough, or the corn is beginning to dry out while you are working.

after floods. Search mostly above the tideline and try to find places which are little known or hard to reach – but be careful not to get trapped by rising tides in small coves. You will find that certain beaches have currents running near them which carry driftwood, while others are comparatively bare. Remember that countless treasures, invisible to any but the initiated, are hidden beneath rotting surfaces. Don't be tempted to leave pieces of wood for picking up on your return, for you can lose many a prize this way.

Don't be too selective when collecting wood.

Many pieces may look uninteresting until they have been worked on. Try to look for unusual shapes and curves, even if they don't resemble any particular form immediately. Try to collect pieces that have variety of color and texture and look for wood with holes, apertures and pieces that protrude, as these are always more exciting to work on. Wood with plenty of rotted surfaces is best, as these can be stripped away easily to reveal the hidden shape of the solid wood beneath.

Take a knife with you when you go searching. Use it to scrape off surface mud which may

*A beautiful boxwood carving of a young gypsy mother and her children. Extremely sharp wood chisels and gouges are needed for the slow carving work. The original shape of the wood has been lost, but because it has weathered so well, the wood has a good color and has not begun to split. Sandpaper and garnetpaper are used for smoothing, and a coat of thinned polyurethane varnish is applied with a soft cloth. After the varnish has hardened, the wood is rubbed down again, polished with beeswax and buffed with lambswool. The base, after careful cleaning and varnishing, provides a rough contrast to the soft, smooth carving mounted on it.*

*These two tall, thin sculptures are made from ivy which grows quite naturally in shapes like these. Let your imagination go to work when deciding what figures or animals it resembles. The black marking on the right-hand figure is caused by natural weathering, and adds greatly to the effect of the finished work.*

be hiding the color, texture and interesting holes. Take a small hand-saw as well, as interesting pieces can be sawn off from fallen tree trunks and root systems. Don't be restricted by the size of a piece of wood, as impressive carvings can be made from pieces of up to 3 m (10 ft) or even larger. It is useful, too, to test the wood first for hardness and grain properties with your pocket knife.

Don't be afraid to make features of embedded rusty nails or brass or copper spikes in wood such as old ships' timbers, as these give an added attraction.

As you gain experience you will develop a sense about the type of wood which will suit your style and what sort of raw material will produce the most rewarding work, but when beginning this craft, be all-encompassing and unrestricted in your collecting. A few early mistakes will teach you far more than unadventurous searching.

*Types of wood*
Good carvings can be made from any type of wood, whether soft or hard, dark- or light-colored. Root wood is one of the best woods to

103

work with, as it is usually hard and waterproof and is found in many interesting shapes. Some roots, for example, branch into two when meeting a rock or stone in the ground, grow round it and then join again, to form a circle of wood which makes a beautiful piece of sculpture.

Ivy, a fairly hard wood that is very resistant to rotting, usually grows on trees which are diseased and in an advanced state of rot. The rotten wood can be hollowed out, leaving intact the fascinating shapes of encircling ivy.

Hardwoods, like oak, rot very slowly in water, leaving a hard core. When the outer rotten wood is removed, the inner core of sound wood is always amazingly intricate and unusual in shape. Forest streams, lakes and ponds are the best places for finding this type of wood.

Soft pinewoods rot so as to give a flaking appearance. They also leave thick wood round the joints between the branches because these parts rot more slowly. You may find, however, when working with pinewoods, that you will have to include some of the very soft wood in the composition, so the sculpture will need to be handled with great care.

Many woods are interesting in color, and have contrasting grain structures which add greatly to the variety of the composition.

*Tools*
Small saw
Pocket knife
Sharp chisels
Gouges
Sharp knife for fine carving
Files and rasps
Wood shaver (usable with one hand, which is useful) for preliminary smoothing
Sandpaper, coarse to smooth grades
A carpenter's vice (vise) (not essential, but useful if you have one)
Piece of glass for final smoothing
Wax polish
Varnish (optional)
Teak oil
Clear epoxy glue

*How to work*
A small piece of wood about 230–300 mm (9–12 in.) long is the most convenient size for a first carving.

Give the wood a good scrub in soapy water, making sure you don't damage any vital part. If the wood is really dirty and requires more cleaning, soak it in fresh water to which bleach or disinfectant has been added. This will remove salt and sterilize the wood.

Allow the wood to dry slowly and naturally by leaving it on a shelf for a few days. The exterior of the driftwood will usually be gray

and rough and may have some bark adhering to it, and some parts may also be soft and rotten. *All* this external material must be removed in order to reveal the true color and grain of the wood underneath. Sometimes you may find that the exciting looking piece of wood with which you started dwindles down to a very dull shape when the rotten wood is removed, and then you must decide whether it is worthwhile going on.

If you have a carpenter's vice (vise), wrap the jaws in cloth or leather, to make sure that they do not mark the wood, and place the work in it.

Steadily and carefully, using sharp chisels, wood carver's tools, files and rasps, carve away the unwanted wood. If you have no vice (vise), hold the wood in one hand, and chisel with the other. (*Note*. To prevent accidents, *always* keep both hands behind the blade of the chisel when working, and *never* work the blade towards your body.)

The important point in carving driftwood is knowing when to stop. This is a matter of artistry and discrimination, which will come with practice. For example, instead of digging all of the softwood out, you may decide to leave

105

some of it, if the shape of the wood seems to call for it. But usually try to get down to the sound heartwood of the piece, as this is the wood which will give the sculpture its character. Work away by gently carving and whittling in very easy stages, rather than hacking and hewing away at it too fast, which will ruin the end result.

When the wood has been carved to your satisfaction, start to smooth away the marks left by the tools. The more careful the original carving, the less smoothing will be needed at this stage. Use a round file, a rasp or a wood shaver to smooth away all the hard edges left by the carving tools. Change to using a smoothing file or a piece of broken glass to complete the rough smoothing. Broken glass is ideal, but take care to wrap it well in cloth or leather to protect your hands. Store bits of broken glass well away from children.

The next stage is to rub down the work before polishing. A lot of time must be given to this in order to achieve a very smooth finish. Rub down with sandpaper, starting with coarse grades, and finishing off with the finest 'wet and dry' paper or garnet paper (grades 120 to 130).

When the sculpture is carved and smoothed, it can be left with a natural finish or it can be waxed or varnished.

*Wax finishing*

Waxing usually gives the best, most natural finish to weathered wood, and a good wax shine is the result of perseverance and effort. Any good wax polish can be used, but the best for this purpose is a solution of white beeswax in warm turpentine. Apply many coats of the wax solution, allowing it to soak into the grain of the wood. Rub the wax into the wood with a cloth and buff it well after each application.

*Alternative finishes*

Driftwood often has a natural gloss resulting

*This sculpture began as an ugly, rotting tree stump with part of the root system attached. It was found on a sandy beach where it had been partly washed and cleaned by the tide. The base was sawn off square so that it would stand upright, and then work began on tidying up the shape of the wood and cleaning out the cracks. Sandpaper was used to give a smooth shape and soften some of the hard, sharp edges, and two coats of wax polish were applied for the final finish.*

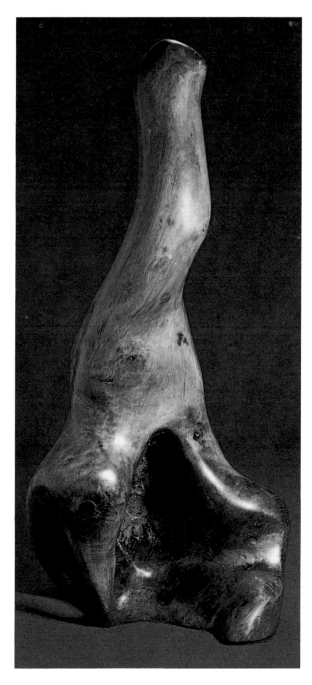

A very bright, high gloss finish can be obtained with varnish. Modern polyurethane varnishes are suitable for this as they don't go yellow with age, and are very hard and durable. You can also buy matt finish polyurethane varnish, for a less glossy result.

When applying varnish, it is important to rub down the wood with the finest garnet papers between each of the first three coats of varnish. Two final coats are usually sufficient, but more coats can be added if required.

Polyurethane varnish can also be used as a rubbed-in grain filler before waxing. Apply the varnish with a fluff-free (lint-free) cloth and rub it into the grain. Allow it to dry, then rub down with the fine garnet paper. Repeat as often as necessary. Applying beeswax after this produces a beautiful polish.

A very quick and useful method of obtaining a finish with wax polish is to use a lambswool mop on an electric drill, a method often used for polishing sculptures.

*Filling in cracks*

Large unwanted cracks can be filled in with beeswax, though in time this will contract and need refilling. Plastic wood can also be used. But take care that the filling does not make your sculpture look too contrived. If filling is necessary, it is better to make up your own matching filler using wood dust and shavings from the piece being carved, mixed with clear glue. When the finish is bright and hard, the sculpture is ready for mounting.

*Mounting*

Many driftwood carvings are complete in themselves and need no mounting, but intricate shapes and abstracts often benefit from mounting on bases upon which they appear to 'float', with the aid of wire or dowelling extensions.

*This hard wood sculpture is the result of a lot of filing and sanding. Although much of the natural shape is lost, in its place are the fine, subtle gradations of color and tone. Where more of the surface is removed, the color becomes lighter. The base is sawn off square and a good shine is the result of much waxing and polishing.*

from beach scouring. In such cases, if the wood has not needed to be carved and smoothed but has been left in its natural state, just a light buffing with a soft cloth will give a pleasing shine.

The staining or painting of driftwood is not recommended as it destroys the natural color, though it is sometimes done where the driftwood is used for flower arranging or home decoration.

# Compatible Materials

| COLORS PAINTS GLUES VARNISH | Water colors | Poster paints | Gouache | Acrylic paints | Synthetic enamel (model paints) | Printer's colors (oil-based) | Printer's colors (water-soluble) | Fiber-tip pens | Clear fast-drying glue (synthetic resin) | Synthetic rubber resin (impact) | PVA glue | Two-part epoxy resin | Acid-free glue | Poly-urethane varnish |
|---|---|---|---|---|---|---|---|---|---|---|---|---|---|---|
| **MATERIALS** | | | | | | | | | | | | | | |
| Bottles and glasses | no | yes | yes | yes | yes | no | no | no | yes | no | no | yes | no | yes |
| Dried flowers | yes | yes | yes | yes | no | no | no | no | yes | no | no | no | yes | no |
| Fabrics | no | no | no | no | no | yes | yes | no | yes | no | yes | no | no | no |
| Feathers | no | no | no | no | no | no | no | no | yes | no | yes | no | yes | no |
| Leaves | no | no | no | no | no | no | no | no | no | no | no | no | yes | no |
| Metals | no | no | no | yes | yes | yes | no | yes | yes | yes | no | yes | no | yes |
| Paper and cardboard | yes | yes | yes | yes | no | yes | yes | yes | yes | yes | yes | yes | no | yes |
| Stones and shells | no | yes | yes | yes | yes | no | no | yes | yes | yes | no | yes | no | yes |
| Wood and seeds | yes | yes | yes | yes | yes | yes | yes | yes | yes | yes | yes | yes | yes | yes |
| Undercoat/ primer | yes | yes | yes | — | with wood: yes | — | — | — | — | — | — | — | — | — |
| Thinner | water | water | water | water | special purpose thinner | white spirit (alcohol) | water | — | — | — | water | — | — | white spirit (alcohol) |
| Lacquer | colorless varnish | colorless varnish or wax | colorless varnish | varnish | — | — | — | varnish | — | — | — | — | — | — |

PLEASE NOTE: This tabular summary is intended only as a rough guide to possibilities. Always follow the instructions and warnings accompanying materials, colors and glues, and whenever possible consult your crafts supplier, art materials dealer and other experts. This is especially important in the case of solvents or thinners and lacquers or varnishes. The composition of materials and paints varies from country to country, and maker to maker. Always try out colors and materials, and all mixtures and solutions before beginning work.

# A Basic Toolkit

**A basic toolkit for all the crafts in this book:**

Apron
Chisels
Files
Hacksaw
Hammer
Knife, craft (with replaceable blades)
Knife, kitchen
Knife, pocket
Paint brushes, 12mm ($\frac{1}{2}$ in.), 25mm (1 in.), fine sable
Palette knife
Pencil
Pins
Pliers
Rasps
Razor blade
Ruler
Sandpaper
Saw, coping
Scissors
Screwdriver
Secateurs (pruning shears)
Straight edge
Toothpicks
Tweezers
Wire-cutters
Wood shaver
Work board
Vice (vise)

# Do's and Don'ts

## Care when working

Always work sharp tools, eg. chisels, away from your body, and keep *both* hands behind the cutting edge.

Always read the instructions on paint cans, glue tubes etc. carefully, and follow safety precautions.

Don't let small children use sharp knives or really strong glues without supervision.

Don't rush to finish a piece of work. Let glue and paint dry really hard before handling. Let dried and pressed flowers, wood and seeds have the time they need to dry out completely, or your finished work will not last.

Keep your work-board tidy when using materials, to avoid marking or damaging your work accidently.

## Preserving nature

Don't collect more material than you really need from plants, bushes or trees.

Don't pull up whole plants with their roots.

Don't tear branches off trees.

Don't pluck feathers from live birds.

Don't trample cornfields or flowerbeds.

Pick flowers carefully, don't damage the parent plant.

Re-use jars, bottles, wood and paper whenever you can.

## Other exciting craft books

If you have enjoyed NATURECRAFT, you will find these books full of interesting ideas and designs for further craft work:

### Colourcraft
### The Beautiful Crafts Book (US title)

A unique and exciting book of colored things to make. The only book that shows you how to use watercolors, poster and oil paints, dyes, color cut-outs, enamels and prints, and how to apply them to almost everything: paper, cloth, wood, cork, copper, tin, linoleum, glass and even stones and eggs. Hundreds of simple ideas, designs and ways of using color to express your natural creativity and imagination. A must for every craftsperson, whether a beginner or a skilled worker.

*128 pp in full color/ISBN 0 85532 363 9 UK. Cased. Search Press/ISBN 0 8069 5366 7 US. Cased. Sterling Publishing Co., Inc.*

### 100 Designs in Pin and Thread
### The Beautiful String Art Book (US title)

A book of ideas, patterns and designs that can be worked in pin and thread (filography). This craft has enormous appeal for people of almost all ages and levels of skill. The designs vary from simple and easy-to-make projects to large, highly-decorative pieces. String art makes wonderful pictures and produces decorative designs for almost every need and location. You can practice the craft in an almost infinite range of colors, sizes, tones and textures. A new adventure for any enthusiast.

*164 pp in full color/ISBN 0 85532 392 2 UK. Cased. Search Press/ISBN 0 8069 5386 1 US. Cased. Sterling Publishing Co., Inc.*

### Magnificent Macramé

A book for the macramé enthusiast who is looking for more ideas and ways of working with string, rope and twine. It begins with simple projects like Christmas tree decorations, bags, plant hangers and belts, and then introduces more adventurous designs including a rainbow-colored hammock, table mats, lampshades, a deckchair and even a hanging cradle for a baby. There are full instructions and illustrations for every project. Color diagrams and close-up color photographs reveal the most intricate parts of the designs.

*144 pp in full color. Search Press/Sterling Publishing Co., Inc.*

### The Christmas Craft Book

A book of enchanting craft ideas and designs for Christmas and other festive occasions. Full instructions, with illustrations and color photographs, are given for a wide range of decorations ranging from candles and nativity scenes to table decorations and straw stars. A special feature of this book is an extensive section on gifts you can make for people of all ages for Christmas, birthdays, anniversaries and other special occasions. These range from a cuddly cub and felt figures to wooden toys and pot-pourris.
This unrivalled guide to designing and making things for Christmas and other feasts should be in every home.

*112 pp in full color. Search Press/Sterling Publishing Co., Inc.*

# Index